D0640982

Here's to a Great Life!

Bryan

Advance Praise for *Be a Winner!*

"When I served as the mayor of the city of Chicago, there was no shortage of people who came to me with ideas about how to strengthen our city. **Bryan is one of the few who had the determination and devotion to turn his idea into a reality for our residents**. I know Bryan not just as a successful businessman and entrepreneur, but as the founder of one of the city's most innovative and transformational social service organizations—the Above and Beyond Treatment Center. It has helped countless Chicagoans get back up on their feet. Bryan is a proven visionary who thinks beyond the boardroom and leverages his success for the benefit of others—and our city is better because of it."

—Rahm Emanuel, Former Mayor of Chicago, Senior Advisor, Centerview Partners

"In an industry best known for sharks, Bryan Cressey has set a different standard for how to be a successful private equity investor. His knowledge, integrity, intuition, and overall passion for healthcare and the entrepreneurs who have brought so many positive changes to it have led him to both financial success and widescale respect from those he encounters. Bryan has used his success to the benefit of many, spawning not only other successful business ventures, but also supporting and even founding charitable organizations that are changing lives one life at a time. As a businessman, investor, philanthropist, and friend, **there is much we can all learn from Bryan about how to live a life that yields success on all fronts**."

—April Anthony, Chief Executive Officer
and Founder, Encompass Health

"Bryan has always generously given his time and resources to support people and causes on which he could have an impact. More than twenty years ago, as a high schooler, I was fortunate to hear Bryan speak. He spoke about his passion for helping entrepreneurs think differently and create meaningful value in their companies. **The enthusiasm and insight he shared that day established my career aspirations and forever changed my trajectory.** Bryan has been an accessible role model ever since, and I continue to find his advice and wisdom invaluable."

—Duane Jackson, Founder and CEO,
Jackson Private Capital

"Bryan Cressey's always active mind absorbs all the incoming; creates a curious mixture of the serendipitous, the light-hearted, and the most profound; digests it all against the backdrop of his rich life experiences; and produces a thought that almost always is tied to action, or transformation, or betterment of others. He is fulfilled by lifting people up, whether it is the young contestant he just vanquished playing air hockey, the least experienced or otherwise ignored person in a boardroom, or the alcoholic who has no hope. **Bryan identifies, embraces, then lifts—to a level of self-empowerment and new energy and a new life.** That's the Bryan Cressey touch."

—Bill Frist, Former United States
Senate Majority Leader

"Bryan has been a friend, partner, and mentor of mine for nearly four decades. Our relationship dates back to 1982 when he made an investment in one of our first healthcare companies. Our journey together has progressed, uninterrupted, for thirty-eight years (and counting) through three companies. Together we have done four IPOs, an LBO, countless acquisitions, raised billions in capital, and employed over 100,000 of our fellow Americans.

"Bryan, in his long career, has flourished as a founder of three of the country's top private equity firms. Through his work, Bryan has distinguished himself as a formidable figure in the healthcare investment sector. On that score, Bryan certainly qualifies as one of the proverbial 'smartest guys in the room.' Decades of experience coupled with an impressive and rare joint degree from Harvard Business School and Harvard Law School certainly proves that. Bryan would be the first to modestly downplay his academic achievements and intellect, and rather credit his reputation and extraordinary success on building relationships and trust with people and companies over the years. I recall in 1996 when my dad and co-founder, Rocco A. Ortenzio, and I went to see Bryan to solicit his support for a new healthcare company we were planning. The 'ask' was not inconsequential in terms of the financial backing, but Bryan said yes even before he had the specifics, projections, and other details. It was a testament to our longstanding and successful relationship, the trust he had in our vision and track record, and why so many people feel a sense of loyalty to Bryan.

"Another hallmark of Bryan's success is his humility and respect for those with whom he works. For nearly four decades, I can honestly say that I never felt as though I 'worked for' Bryan. He would often say that good decisions or investments were the result of smart management teams, and for less successful deals, he would take the sole responsibility for the decision.

"It is almost cliché that private equity is a series of well-timed, relatively short-term investments with a constant eye on the 'exit' or 'liquidity' event. Often and understandably, the private equity owner has a bias for growth over infrastructure or longterm corporate strategy. This is another area where Bryan has set himself apart. **I have never worked with a private equity investor who is more committed to a company's long-range vision, values, and culture.** Bryan appreciates, promotes, and supports building value in his companies through a culture of employee engagement, quality of service, and value-based leadership. He is a testament to the very best qualities a private equity partner has to offer.

"Bryan also has an innate ability to assess and evaluate talent and leaders. He knows the distinct difference between a manager and a leader—those who people will follow versus others who you work for. I believe Bryan would further refine the definition of a leader as one who helps others succeed. That is a lesson from Bryan that I carry forward every day. By that standard, Bryan is a remarkable leader who has helped hundreds of leaders and companies succeed throughout his career.

"In closing, for owners or entrepreneurs considering partnering with Bryan, I share these two takeaways that I have come to recognize over the years. First, Bryan never makes an investment about him. Rather, it is always about the company, its employees, customers, and other stakeholders. Second, Bryan might not have the most to say on any particular topic, but when he does speak I highly recommend you listen closely. **There is always tremendous value, insight, and wisdom in his view.** I am very pleased that Bryan has written this book. It will be an invaluable source of wisdom that we can learn from and use throughout our lives."

—Robert A. Ortenzio, Executive Chairman and Co-Founder, Select Medical

BE A WINNER!

LIFE'S HANDBOOK *for*
JOY *and* SUCCESS

BRYAN C. CRESSEY

POST HILL PRESS

A POST HILL PRESS BOOK
ISBN: 978-1-64293-894-4
ISBN (eBook): 978-1-64293-895-1

Be a Winner!:
Life's Handbook for Joy and Success
© 2021 by Bryan C. Cressey
All Rights Reserved

Cover art by Cody Corcoran
Illustrations by Juvenal Martinez

Although every effort has been made to ensure that the personal and professional advice present within this book is useful and appropriate, the author and publisher do not assume and hereby disclaim any liability to any person, business, or organization choosing to employ the guidance offered in this book.

No part of this book may be reproduced, stored in a retrieval system, or transmitted by any means without the written permission of the author and publisher.

Post Hill Press
New York • Nashville
posthillpress.com

Published in the United States of America
1 2 3 4 5 6 7 8 9 10

To my incredible parents, Charles and Lorraine,
who lovingly gave me remarkable freedom. I became
me, I learned the Universe, then became them.

CONTENTS

How Life Really Works

I was picked up at the airport by a CEO sporting a strong reputation in an area of interest to our investment firm. He kindly offered to drive me to his office for our in-person meeting. Knowing he was an industry leader, I struck up a conversation to learn more about his background. He had been chairman of the industry association, so he was very well-known and admired. This CEO had run a company in the business and was seeking to build a new company in the same sector, which he understood extremely well. All sounded positive.

Five minutes later, when the CEO turned his car into the parking lot of the office building, I knew he was going to fail. How did I know that? It was based on experience, not logic. And it's one of the hundreds of lessons in this book, all of which I've learned from experience. What I observed is that he drove extremely cautiously. He drove below the speed limit and slowed down for green stoplights, knowing they might possibly turn yellow. He flunked my driving test. Why did the way he drove consign him to failure?

Here's the reason: he was obviously very cautious; he drove almost as in fear.

A person who behaves based on fear and is overly cautious will never be able to build a successful start-up company. I've seen this driving test flunked numerous times and have consistently been rewarded by not investing in that individual's company.

Over the ensuing six months, this CEO succeeded in raising the money for his new company, and he did so from a well-known investment firm. On paper, the situation looked very good. Yet within a year, the investment firm had to write off their investment as a loss! I was very lucky that I was considering not only logic, but also the clues I look for in a leader's emotional and personal characteristics. Those clues foretell the future.

Are You Interested in Being a Winner?

This book imparts numerous simple ways I've discovered to succeed in life, from personal fulfillment and joy, to business and entrepreneurship.

Be A Winner! is the one book I wish I had when I graduated from school. I've been fortunate to help build successful companies (and some not!) for forty years as a venture capital and private equity investor; I've also partnered with management teams to grow some great companies. We have consistently achieved investment returns exceeding 20 percent compounded per year. I've been fortunate to spot unique opportunities and recruit management to create and build new companies as well.

I've learned so many important things from working with talented managers and my astounding teammates that I'm full of gratitude for my good fortune, and I'd like to help your life turn out the same way.

The keys to being a winner are in the next pages. Good luck, and enjoy the amazing life you can have!

How to Create Your
Wonderful Life

How can you change your life toward greatness?

Happiness? We'll start here, with nineteen ways I've learned to become successful:

1. Plan backward. This sounds odd, but it works. Most people plan their lives one step at a time, thinking only about their next forward moves or their next objectives.

Why I contend this is wrong is that the way to truly succeed is to look to where you wish to be at the pinnacle of an accomplishment in the future, and to plan backward in logical steps, to where you are today. It works like when we were kids and worked on solving those maze puzzles on paper, where we found the pathway by working backward.

We started at the end and worked backward to see the proper steps. Plan backward from several moves ahead and you see your path.

Planning backward

An example of where I planned backward was when I had a dream of creating a new future of successful addiction healing. Experiences in my family and our world caused me to long for better answers for suffering individuals and families. I sensed a desperate need for effective addiction healing. I envisioned what this might look like in the future and planned backward from there.

In my vision, I saw four primary dreams: producing better outcomes for patients with new treatment methods, transforming patients for a lifetime (not just short-term), providing a model for the future of addiction healing, and providing that better care to the poor and homeless for free.

Planning backward:

1. From the vision above, a lifetime of transformation requires changing entire lives—not only becoming sober, but getting housing, jobs, and being reunited with families.
2. Producing better outcomes and life transformation requires creating a new treatment philosophy that functions better than the older model
3. Reinventing these things requires evidence and research into which care modalities and teachings could produce these improvements
4. Therefore, we need innovators from the field to get excited about changing today's difficulties into tomorrow's successes
5. Treating the poor and homeless requires locating in their neighborhood so they can take the sidewalk to a better life

6. Described above are major changes and innovations which demand great, talented leaders to manage these processes into success. Of course, attracting great leaders requires an inspiring vision, which attracts these terrific and innovative individuals to attempt this revolution.

7. Therefore, I must create and communicate a magnetic vision, and then I must describe and speak my vision with great enthusiasm and belief. Action: Number 7 above was where I started enactment of this vision in 2015.

Result: Reread the vision paragraph above starting with, "In my vision," and all you read there has now come to fruition. Above and Beyond is now well-known to world experts. Internationally recognized expert and author of twelve books on addiction treatment, Dr. Stanton Peele has stated, "Above and Beyond is a modern treatment miracle…in a field badly in need of one." And two-time *New York Times* bestselling author of books on addiction and its treatment, Johann Hari has said, "What you have here at Above and Beyond is the model that should replace the broken addiction treatment model in the U.S." In its fifth year, Above and Beyond has received a national award for its new treatment program, and it has also received a national Best and Brightest Companies to Work For® award for featured in the *Wall Street Journal* in 2021.

Why does planning backward work? It works because humans cannot fly: we cannot fly from the bottom to the top of a hill. We can only climb that hill one step at a time. But for large dreams, we usually cannot see a path to the top—we may try one step, encounter difficulty or frustration, and give up—because we don't see the way forward!

Planning backward gives us the steps. The pathway we can take. And planning backward one step at a time to the beginning gives us each step to take, from the beginning to accomplishment. We can then take those steps and achieve dreams and visions. It may not be easy, and we'll need to persevere, but we're more able to do so knowing we're on our pathway to the top.

Do all your large planning backward!

2. Aim high! You will probably be positively surprised by what you can accomplish. I personally wanted to do something very unusual and be very successful, or fail trying. Taking some *risks* in your career increases your odds of success greatly. Many people fear taking any risks in their lives or careers and are rarely positively surprised by where they land. A quote from the famous philosopher Duke Snyder—actually, Duke was the right fielder for the Brooklyn Dodgers in the 1950s. He said, "Swing hard, you might hit the ball."

3. Mistakes. My greatest education has not come from school, but from my mistakes. These will never be your most popular teacher, but they can be outstanding. I make lots of mistakes and learn from them. When we're young, we try to hide mistakes or deny them. But *life* and *success* are trial and error. Life is more fun, and much easier, when you admit mistakes and learn from them.

After graduation from school, life turns 180 degrees, and most persons don't recognize that. It changes in this crucial way: During school, to achieve top grades, one must make no mistakes on the tests. And we are taught that all the way through our childhood into young adulthood. "No mistakes."

I have observed that after graduation, life suddenly changes: now it's the *opposite*—he or she who makes the most mistakes wins! Why? Because learning to succeed in a job or building a company is a trial-and-error process. Note the many successful entrepreneurs who have failed many times and then succeeded.

If you learn from your mistakes, you want to make plenty of them, because each mistake is a new teacher to you; and after making enough mistakes, having many teachers, you learn enough to grow very successfully! The key is admitting mistakes and learning from them. Life is much happier, and much more exciting, using this process.

4. Humility. We have a human instinct to think we're smart, which can backfire if we don't transcend it. In a venture capital investment I made early in my career, the CEO and I were at dinner, and he was telling me about some operating difficulties they were having. I offered ideas of what to do, and I noticed he was writing notes on what I said. My first thought was, "Wow, I'm smart," and then I thought, "I shouldn't be giving advice since I'm not smart at operations, and neither is he if he's taking notes! He doesn't know what he's doing!" That sadly proved correct as the company eventually failed. Humility allows learning, and learning drives success in all you do.

5. Be *creative*. Devise some creative ways to help your firm break some new ground in your first couple years. Don't accept the way things are done as the optimal way; mentally question *everything* significant. In my experience, you can generally improve on *what* is done and *how* it's done.

6. Before deciding the next job you want, carefully figure out what your goals and values are, i.e., what you *live to do*. Figure out where in society and the economy you can do what you really love, and where you can create a large positive impact. Then speak with practitioners in the field and really understand it. If it's what you love and enjoy, you will succeed.

7. Associate with great people. Choose to work with an outstanding mentor who will teach you how to succeed in your chosen endeavor. If you can find a mentor who is partly entrepreneurial, you will learn how to create change successfully. One of our great CEOs taught me an important lesson: excellent CEOs don't want "good"; they want "great"! They won't settle for good. In a 1970s cable TV investment we made, after a

positive first year, our CEO told me he was going to replace the chief operating officer. I was surprised because I thought he was good and doing a fine operating job. The CEO told me, "He is pretty good—but I want great if we're going to build a great company." That CEO developed a talented and motivated team and built an extremely successful and valuable company!

8. The next key to success is the least recognized. Believe it or not, the biggest key to your success is not to become the most skilled person possible; it's this: *pick the right industry*, or profession, to participate in. The secret is to get in an area with enough growth, profitability, and possibilities to create great opportunities for you.

9. Choose your direction, and timing, thoughtfully. Years ago, when I completed my servitude as a student, many of my friends, even some who were otherwise intelligent, headed into the then-popular business of real estate development and banking. These businesses are highly cyclical. Entering at the peak of a cycle, those friends had an eventful twelve months: graduation, first job, recession, termination.

10. Impose *your* judgment on the world. Don't let others tell you what you should do with your life. Decide for yourself. This will enable you to create *your* world more as you want it to be—*not* as others hand it to you. Looking forward in grad school, I didn't see careers that excited me; none fit my own passions. Luckily, I learned about the new field of venture capital from a speaker at school, and I knew that was what I wanted to do—finally, something that fit me. I worked hard to get into the nascent industry: only two people were hired into venture capital nationwide that year, and I felt very lucky to be one of them.

11. Have fun in your work. The world is *not* a priori serious. Some people make it that way. Some people think they must act

seriously to be thought learned and capable. What a mistake! They miss life's joy and aren't thought smarter than those who show the confidence of being funny. Just avoid using humor that embarrasses anyone…who is present in the room.

12. Act with integrity always. Good things will come to you when people trust you. And as Mark Twain recommended, "Always do right. That will gratify some of the people, and astonish the others." And you will be more successful if you have high ethical standards of conduct for yourself. Why? Because cheating to attain your objective means not pushing yourself to be the best. It's like lowering the crossbar in the high jump: you won't force yourself to learn to jump higher. It's exactly the same with ethics: keeping the bar higher forces you to learn to be better, and you will. We had a competitor to one of our businesses that paid off their customers' employees to get business. Our company lost an occasional piece of business to that competitor. But our company became better than the other company, won most of the business, and grew rapidly; the other company stagnated because it hadn't pushed itself to improve. Regarding a questionable situation, a good maxim to follow is, "If you have to ask, you already know the answer." In other words, if it's in the gray zone, don't go there. To maintain a great reputation, you need to avoid even the appearance of possible impropriety. Perception becomes reality.

Here's another example of what happens when people let themselves go wrong. I call it, "Easy come, easy go." I've seen several individuals that apparently didn't feel inside themselves that they had earned their wealth virtuously. To some, their money came overly easily from simply being in the right place at the right time. They spent and lost their money exceedingly quickly. Personal integrity. They didn't feel they had earned the money. It's far better to earn less and feel great about it than to cut corners and feel ruined inside.

At a partners' meeting one week, we were discussing various potential investments. One of the partners described a technology company in California that sounded quite incomplete and risky to the other partners, so the majority suggested the opportunity not be pursued. The partner suggesting the investment looked a little pained as he told the rest of us, "I was at the company last week and I shook hands on a deal with the CEO." In unison, the other partners responded, "Then we're in!" We all believe in strong ethics and values in conducting business, and in our lives. Unfortunately, the majority was right and the company didn't succeed, so we lost our money. Ow! But it was the right thing to do.

13. Don't be in a hurry to succeed. I've seen many individuals that are so compelled to succeed fast that they fail. How? Because they jump from thing to thing, believing each one will propel them to the top—they never do anything long enough to become truly good at it. Don't be in a hurry; take time to become great at what you enjoy.

And don't be in such a hurry to evaluate your own wins and losses. The unexpected will sometimes happen, as this story demonstrates:

We once made an investment in an early-stage computer technology company, and it didn't go well: over several years, the company encountered disappointment after disappointment. We valued the company at only one dollar in our reports and assumed we had lost our money. Sixteen years after making the investment, we received a phone call that the company had finally become successful—in fact, extremely successful—and it was being sold for a huge amount. That small single investment, which was one of forty-eight investments in our $60 million fund, returned almost $40 million, so the seemingly failed small company returned almost the entire fund to investors!

Another time, we invested in a medical company that significantly underperformed during its first couple years. The company was publicly traded, and its stock went from nine dollars per share to twenty-seven cents. It was in default with banks and was nearly out of cash. The board of directors had fifteen meetings one spring trying to help, then we received an offer to buy the company at fifty cents per share, or a total of $60 million. The board said "No, but we'll take $67 million."

The buyer became emotional and responded poorly—he got angry at our board and CEO and walked away. We had luckily begun to see one ray of sunshine through the clouds at that point, so we stood firm. Our company's new CEO got the sales growing, and then growing rapidly.

The stock price rose from twenty-seven cents to four dollars by year-end, and the company began generating positive cash flow. With great leadership by the CEO, the stock rose to ninety dollars per share in a few years, and after our anguishing difficulties, it turned into a highly successful investment for us. Everyone but the potential buyer was extremely glad that we were resolute during the storm, and our new captain sailed out the other side of the tempest. The potential buyer lost an outstanding opportunity by becoming emotional and overruling the logical decision he had initially made to buy.

14. Some may feel that this point is bad news: it's that money does *not* buy happiness. Period. I've been without money, and had lots of it, and I guarantee you it doesn't correlate much with happiness. Figure out what you want to do with your life that you'll find satisfying, gratifying, and do it. I entered the venture capital business because it sounded excitingly right for me. And it was! I joined the venture group at First Chicago and was introduced to an interesting situation. Three years before I joined firm, my teammates at First Chicago had made an investment in a start-up company called Federal Express, whose breakthrough idea was to bring all shipments to one location in the nation before distributing items to the destination city.

Previously, items had been shipped directly from each city to another city, but that required thousands of daily flights between city pairs. The idea that founder Fred Smith created while in college was that by flying all packages to one location, the number of flights to deliver all items would be greatly reduced, lowering costs and improving delivery service. When I arrived at First Chicago in 1976, the investment in Federal Express had been in deep financial trouble due to the 1974 oil embargo, which increased oil prices by four times! The fuel costs almost drove FedEx bankrupt. In fact, two years after the original venture capital investment, the company was going to miss payroll on a Friday, which could mean the end for the company; and believing it to be a lost cause, many original investors would not invest money to save it. On a Thursday in 1974, the day before the employees needed paid, a few of the venture investment firms wired money to keep the company alive. That small investment, totaling only 17 percent of the money originally invested, bought 87 percent of the venture ownership in Federal Express. Because the company's plight placed it near death, nobody would invest at a higher price, and many firms chose not to invest even at this low price. Our firm invested in that low-price round because it saw that even though Federal Express was raising prices, the company's shipment volumes continued growing, so our firm reasoned there must be strong demand for this new overnight shipment service.

In 1978, when Federal Express was quite profitable and growing very well, I ran into one of the bank lenders to the company. The bank had loaned the money in 1973 and went through the difficult period of 1974—1976 with the company. The conversation went something like this:

Me: "Jack, isn't Federal Express a wonderful growth company?"

Jack: "No; it's terrible. We almost lost our money loaning to them!"

Me: "Yes, but it's doing great now—very profitable and growing very well, and it's passing up the established air freight companies."

Jack: "It's still a rotten company."

Me: "Well, we own lots of stock in Federal Express, and it's become a wonderful investment for us! Why are you so negative about the company?"

Jack: "It almost lost our bank's money—that's always a bad company."

The lesson: think flexibly! *Don't* let your early impression of something or someone become your permanent impression! Watch for new evidence and change your ideas. In this case, Jack was inflexibly stuck on his early opinion and could never see that Federal Express was becoming a great company. Jack would not have taken the stock if we gave it to him! Yet our firm made around twenty times its investment in Federal Express. And if Jack had recognized the future promise FedEx had and bought stock then, today he would have made 228 times his investment!

15. Specialize in something. Even a narrow specialty is a big market in our world's economy. Winners are those who become the best at something.

One summer, I was reviewing a possible investment in a behavioral school company that was known to be clinically outstanding. I even checked its reputation with my dad, who was an MSW, and he was quite positive on the company's reputation for quality. Their growth and financial results were good too. The CEO running the company for the family that owned it was a little weak, though, and a young new executive from outside the company was planning to take over with the family's approval. As I spoke to the new CEO, it was evident he wished to enter several new businesses to grow the company faster. However, as I probed, I learned that he had never operated any businesses like these, so I thought it would be folly to enter those new businesses. Later, when we were seated together on a flight, I shared my thoughts with the older CEO who was running the company for the family. I explained that they already had a wonderful business at which they were the best and could grow successfully. In response, I suggested they not enter any new businesses but instead concentrate on growing where they were winning.

The CEO told me he couldn't see why it would matter. And I told him, "When you're mining for gold, and you discover a wide, deep vein of gold, you mine it! You don't waste your time going to dig at other locations—you have what every other miner dreams of. And your current business is exactly that deep, wide vein of gold. Just mine it."

I was quite surprised when he couldn't understand that. I declined to invest, but other firms did, and the new CEO spent the company's money on the new ventures, which all failed. Sadly, the entire company, including the great behavioral business, went bankrupt.

When you find the gold, focus on mining it!

16. Impress every person, every time you meet. It will enhance your reputation, and you'll quickly gain more responsibility.
17. Figure out how your firm's success is measured—and contribute more to that success than is expected of you.

18. Never fall into a rut. Examine constantly whether you are doing what you want. Here's an example and warning:

I learned an important lesson while working for a conveyor belt company while in college. The business was quite small—there were only five employees, including me. One was an older man (in his sixties) who worked in the office, doing the product purchasing, taking phone orders, and sending the bills to customers. As I got to know him better, he shared a sad story about his life with me. "Bob" told me that he had started in this business thirty-five years ago, and had planned to leave it soon to do something he loved; he had never loved this job.

But at first, he had kids, so he didn't make the move, and then he had a mortgage, and it then seemed like the next moment he was sixty-four years old and had never made the move he wished to make. Therefore, he had never done what he loved, and now couldn't because he was nearing retirement. This was a vivid lesson to me: you must proactively avoid settling into a rut. If you don't think about that occasionally and check what you are doing, it may happen to you and lead to permanent disappointment and sadness in your life. What we regularly do becomes a routine, and a routine can become a rut we may remain in unless we exercise a little paranoia and assertively assess whether we are letting parts of our life travel in a rut. We must proactively change and grow rather than passively letting life happen to us.

19. Success goes not to the person who works the longest hours, but to the person who gets their most important things done. Prioritize!

Private Equity Adventures

In the 1970s, we co-invested with the KKR partners in an early leveraged buyout, and the company was grading some land for a new plant when an explosion occurred—it appeared to be from the dirt being graded, and it was powerful enough to blow the Caterpillar tractor over! Our team approached the large conglomerate that had sold the land and they denied anything was wrong with the property, but when our team pointed out that the dirt kept exploding, the sellers finally admitted they had buried pyrophoric materials (chemicals that explode when exposed to air) on the land!

Our company received a nice settlement…and some nonexplosive land.

ENTREPRENEURSHIP

Entrepreneurship is really magical!

Since cofounding our first venture capital firm in 1980, I have benefitted from the positive power of entrepreneurship. These powers create the abilities to build companies, innovate widely, create visions and achieve them, and inspire other talented persons to the join and drive adventurous accomplishments.

Entrepreneurship is one of the most important and timely characteristics to think about in your life. First, entrepreneurship is probably the most powerful force in American business today. Entrepreneurship has brought us several companies that within twenty years of their founding reached the largest market value of any company in the world! Microsoft, founded by now-iconic entrepreneurs, surpassed the venerable General Electric, Exxon Mobil, and every other company in 1998. Cisco rose to exceed all companies in market value in

2001—within its first twenty years. Google reached number one by size in 2016, and in 2020, Apple and Amazon reign. These successes are incredible accomplishments! And they demonstrate the forces unleashed by entrepreneurial processes.

Most successful companies in the U.S. today were founded by entrepreneurs only one generation ago. I cofounded my first private equity company in 1980 with two partners and four cardboard boxes. Today, the companies we have invested in, own, and are building employ tens of thousands of people and have billions in revenues. This is not due to my capability—it is due to the magic of entrepreneurship. There is certainly a company being founded right now that in twenty years will reach the highest market value of all U.S. companies! Can you spot it? Entrepreneurship is powerful, and it is most alive and successful in America.

Another reason to discuss entrepreneurship is change: change creates opportunities (or problems, depending which side of it you're on). If you're proactive, change can mean opportunity. And change is accelerating constantly in the world economy. For a moment, think about and answer this question for yourself: Why has America been the most successful developed economy in the world? The U.S. has been the fastest growing fully developed economy on earth. And consider what the U.S. has working against it today.

First, we are a higher cost producer of products than most economies we compete against (because we enjoy high earnings, a high standard of living, and our health care is expensive, so we're high cost). Also working against the U.S. is our educational system; forty years ago, it was probably the finest in the world. It is now ranked fifteenth or so in the world and slipping. In a knowledge-based economy, this is a large and growing handicap.

So, with a high-cost economy and an underperforming educational system, why does the U.S. grow faster than other mature economies?

The U.S. succeeds in spite of its handicaps because of entrepreneurship! How does that work? We tolerate and accept failure better than any other country. In the U.S., people can start companies that fail, then start one that is highly successful, and this is a common or even predominant pattern. Yet in numerous cultures, and in many large economies, business failure brings shame on the individual and even on their family. That douses entrepreneurial spirits! In America, we celebrate entrepreneurship, understand failures, and move on. Perhaps it's Abe Lincoln's example of consistent failure before he became one of history's greatest leaders that acculturated us to persevere to success. As author Robert Kiyosaki notes, "Losers quit when they fail…Winners fail until they succeed."

America has led the world in entrepreneurship. This has created the highest level of inventions, new technologies, and successful companies worldwide. Consistently. Here are some facts: although firms with fewer than twenty employees (small firms) represent only 18 percent of U.S. employment, they are responsible for 53 percent of total job creation! Over half of new jobs!

Famed economist Joseph Schumpeter first recognized the crucial role of the entrepreneur. He argued that innovation by the entrepreneur led to gales of "creative destruction," as innovations caused old inventories, ideas, technologies, skills, and equipment to become obsolete. This creative destruction, he taught, caused continuous progress and improved standards of living for everyone.

So, if entrepreneurship, which can occur in any size company, from a start-up to Amazon, is the key to large achievements, how can you and I accomplish it?

Entrepreneurship is two simple actions—1) searching for, and 2) acting on—opportunities.

Opportunities are mostly created by change.

Here are four reasons to consider some creative action for yourself. First, change is driving entrepreneurial opportunities. Second, the payoff is large to people and companies involved. Third, it's fun! And fourth, entrepreneurship is challenging and rewarding.

To successfully entrepreneur within a company, do the following:

Start with a look around, noting your competitive landscape and observing the things that are moving. Author Robert Heller says "Researchers in the field of entrepreneurship believe that opportunity recognition behavior is the most basic and important entrepreneurial behavior."

When you see what is moving and changing, ask yourself: Are the drivers of this change temporary? Or are these real increasing trends? Follow those and develop your plans around them.

The second step is to experiment. Try new services or products on a small scale to see what works best, how to communicate to customers best, and what the customers like best. Once you've done this small-scale testing, determine whether it might be worth introducing more widely by looking at the following: the return on your capital invested, customer enthusiasm, how you could best organize to deliver it, what human resources are required, and whether it would utilize a similar organization to the way you do business now. Would it disrupt your current organization? In that case, separate it into another company or go slower. Then ask how does all this compare to your other opportunities?

If your new opportunity looks good, ask how much growth your organization can absorb while remaining healthy and strong. Don't try to grow beyond that pace. It will depend partly on how solid your business's foundation is, the quality of people, IT systems, and the quality of teamwork and communication existing within your firm.

Which of the following two assertions do you personally believe is most important: maximizing the percentage of decisions you get right, or alternatively, making and implementing decisions more quickly? For successful entrepreneurship, it's number two. Successful entrepreneurs run a series of experiments and learn from them. Entrepreneurship is trying a bunch of things and seeing what works, then implementing that. The world is usually too complex and uncertain to try and predict a priori—like Descartes—what things are like. We have to experiment.

Too many of us confuse unsuccessful experiments with something we might view as a negative—mistakes. Yet the key to success is learning from mistakes, recognizing them as experiments, and learning from them. Many people don't learn from mistakes; in fact, many don't take responsibility for their mistakes. But if I'm always blaming the mistake on someone else, or some outside factor, I *cannot learn* from it. I have seen that people who are successful take responsibility for their foul-ups. For example, one our CEOs, Tim Burfield, was always humble and even critical of his own leadership efforts. He credited his colleagues for successes, himself for failures, and built a highly successful public company. When a division turned unprofitable, another CEO named Rocky Ortenzio moved (at age sixty-five) to live at the division for six weeks to fix it. It was stressful and involved a lot of firing and hiring, but he did it because he viewed it as *his* foul-up, having the wrong people there in the first place. Today, he is extremely successful—partially because he's admitted mistakes and fixed situations. Here's a new quote for you: "To err is human; to err and learn is entrepreneurial."

Research shows that entrepreneurs, contrasted with managers, function quite differently: they act in the face of more uncertainty than ordinary managers. Action—not excess study—is their key to create progress. Think if you waited for perfect information, not wanting to make a mistake, and therefore took action every five years—versus a competitor who looks at the situation, uses their judgment and experience to decide, and then acts and is right 70 percent of the time, and learns from their mistakes when they aren't right. Guess which one vastly outperforms and which style fails as a leader. Today, in fast-changing markets, the opportunity for success usually disappears before rational/analytical decision-making can be conducted. And is our world changing faster or slower? Faster—thus the constantly increasing need for faster, more entrepreneurial decision-making style for all of us.

Research by Busenitz and Barney has shown that using econometric decision-making modes will not only postpone decisions until too late, but it will often or usually result in wrong decisions!

Here's how I describe the key ways entrepreneurs do things differently from ordinary managers:

> Entrepreneurs figure out how to overcome obstacles; non-entrepreneurs allow obstacles to stop them.
>
> Entrepreneurs remember the *goals*; non-entrepreneurs remember the *rules*.
>
> Entrepreneurs are passionate; non-entrepreneurs are stolid.
>
> Entrepreneurs care about progress; non-entrepreneurs care about conformance.
>
> Entrepreneurs see what's wrong with the world; non-entrepreneurs don't care.

You may think, as I used to think about myself, that you're not creative enough to be entrepreneurial. However, studies have shown that creativity can be developed. The most effective way to hone this skill is before making a decision, make a large list of many options, even unattractive ones and far-out ones; this will broaden your idea horizon and improve your decision-making, *and* you'll learn to think more creatively as a habit.

To succeed at entrepreneurship, you must assume some risk. I've observed that most people take too little risk in life, yet the economy and society reward risk-taking. Most of my friends who have taken risks have succeeded. Most who have not succeeded in life got stuck in life; they weren't happy but were afraid to change their situation. Here's one example of a risk-averse would-be entrepreneur: we invested in a company that set out to buy and operate newspapers in the early

1990s, but the CEO was so cautious, he only bought two tiny papers in the Dakotas, and he failed to take advantage of a great opportunity. We lost half our money. During a great epoch of value creation and fortunes in newspapers, his company went nowhere—because he was afraid to take any risk.

Here are some other things we've learned about entrepreneurship and building companies. Looking back over the most successful companies we have built, I found they follow a similar formula.

Our best companies improve the quality of products or services offered, they market and sell more heavily to increase market share, and they cut costs continuously.

This can lead to an unassailable market position: being a low-cost producer with top quality, and a happy, growing customer base.

So, here's a summary of how an entrepreneur might start and build a successful new company:

1. Establish the long-term direction and vision.
2. Allocate planned growth between acquisitions where that's appropriate and internal growth where that's better.
3. Get outstanding people and motivate them.
4. Continuously improve operations.
5. Gain scale economies.
6. Extend product and service lines through development.
7. Remember that the highest quality wins. Our home-run investments are almost always in companies that follow this formula.

PRIVATE EQUITY ADVENTURES

Early in my career, we had just helped start a cable television company with a soon-to-be-great executive, Steve Dodge, and we were driving in a pickup truck up a mountainside to see the antenna headend at the top. Being the youngest, I didn't get the first-class ride: I stood in the bed of the pickup truck and Steve was speeding around a corner on the dirt mountain road when at the last moment, I saw a large tree branch about to take my head off and ducked barely in time so the wind just parted my hair. I told Steve he almost killed me, and he just laughed and laughed—life is Darwinian, I guess. I survived to see Steve and his team build a great company with us.

Learning the Lessons

I awakened Thursday, July 28, 2012 in a surprising place—drinking coffee in a room at the Santa Barbara Inn. I gazed across the attractively uneven dark planking through white lace curtains to a sunny blue sky. The prior afternoon, I had expected to be heading from Chicago to my home in Barrington on the commuter train, but I was jolted by an unexpected call with unwanted news. The news hurt. It sounded irreversible, but I wondered, half in a daze, whether anything positive might be done. The message was that the agreement we had worked on tirelessly for eight months to invest in an attractive Santa Barbara company we had wanted for our portfolio had fallen apart. The two owners of the company had decided not to go forward and told my partner their decision was firm and final.

Instead of the commuter train home, I rushed to the airport and flew to Santa Barbara, uninvited. I knew the owners were having dinner together Wednesday evening, and I wanted to arrive in town in time to call them at their dinner, tell them I'm in town, and ask whether I might join them. I did just that. It failed.

They said no thanks. However, in saying no, they felt a little guilty, because I had flown across the country and was near their restaurant when they said no to me. They invited me to join them at the company's office in the morning, reminding me however there was no hope of salvaging the deal because their decision was final.

I moved slowly out of my bed Thursday morning, thinking about different possible approaches to help them decide they wanted to change their "irreversible decision." I gradually realized that telling them reasons they should change their decision would not work, so I hit on a very different approach to try.

When I arrived at the company, a cute and frisky little dog greeted me as I walked through the modular office space toward the CEO's office. I smiled at my unexpected single friend, the dog, and entered. The CEO and chairman sat in two chairs, wearing stern countenances, and offered me the couch, where I sat as they both stared at me. I greeted them, and they reminded me this was only a social visit, as there was no business to discuss. I realized I must take the lead immediately and roll out my game plan.

I started with positivity, and I tried to deepen the emotional relationship we had with each other: "It's great to be with you again, and I've always enjoyed our times together, so thanks for allowing me one more visit this morning." I had decided I would simply listen to what had changed their minds on completing our transaction together. I would just listen, with acceptance and no resistance to their thinking, if they were willing to tell me anything.

I offered, "I'm so sorry our partnership didn't work out, because I think we would have all enjoyed helping grow your software company together, and I understand we won't be doing that, but since we're together, and I think we mutually like and respect each other, I would greatly appreciate it, for my education and to help me improve in the future, if you could share what we might have done differently than what we did that led you to your final decision? Our firm has many areas we can improve in, and since we're visiting together, I would personally be very grateful if you might help me improve our firm as we go forward."

The chair responded, "We admire you flying here just to visit, knowing there's no deal here, so I'll at least share some observations we have, and our perspectives on several things." I relaxed and just listened for the next couple hours, simply responding with some questions so I could understand more deeply what they had seen and thought during recent discussions.

I began to understand what they were feeling. And I thought of a couple possible solutions to the things bothering them, but I listened for two and a half hours before bringing those up. One of those suggestions involved me spending more time with the two of them as we partnered in building their company into a great future. I also sensed that their original expectation was that they would receive from us senior-level guidance and discussions, and they were sensing they would mostly be working with younger people in our firm. I recognized they were disappointed by that. Another emotion they felt from that? I recognized they were feeling hurt—probably thinking that maybe we didn't view them as important enough to receive more senior level attention. Neither of those thoughts were accurate, as we viewed them and their company as extremely important, but in relationships, reality does not matter—their feelings constitute reality and their feelings were valid—so rather than being dismissive or argumentative, to achieve good dialogue on the emotional level, I primarily listened.

We had talked for three hours, and I had waited two hours and thirty minutes before I made any suggestions at all. I went to a level above what they expected in seeking a high level of senior attention and time by offering to serve with them on their board of directors. They were excited by that. Next, I promised that my partner and I would be available to listen, talk, and share ideas together anytime they wished (so they would receive plenty of time from the more experienced and senior people in our firm). They believed me on this promise because I had believed them regarding their emotions and what they desired. I could never have intuited what they would want without listening deeply for a couple of hours and authentically caring about them and their needs.

I was there to listen.

We became partners, and the company increased its capabilities even further, gained more customers whom they made happy, and the investment did well for them and for us. It was a wonderful experience, and one that was nearly lost.

How did I reach the decision to simply listen? I knew that their decision was an emotional one, not relying on logic but solely on emotions. How could I know that? Because we had previously agreed on the price of the investment, and the terms of the deal, the specific logical details had been accepted and agreed upon by both parties. I was contending with their feelings and perceptions, probably from communications during the investment process.

Emotions are valid. They are as important as logic. Decisions may be based on logic or emotion, or a combination of the two. And if you wish to have a decision changed, you must first understand how it was made. Emotions must be understood and discussed differently than logic.

How do you best deal with others' emotions? Here are four steps:

First, you listen earnestly. You just listen. You don't argue or point out things to them. Secondly, while you listen, you pretend to be the speaker, not yourself. You put yourself in their shoes—feeling their emotions and understanding them. You won't be able to communicate with them emotionally unless you achieve the state of *feeling* their emotion from their perspective. Third, you genuinely feel bad that they experienced those emotions, be they sadness, disrespect, fear, anger, or other feelings. Fourth, you then express your disappointment, with empathy, that they experienced those emotions.

Those feelings they communicated in that office were unpleasant and made them not want to partner with us, and I was able to internalize that unpleasantness in myself because I listened and genuinely cared for them. When you are authentically concerned, others will sense that—then and only then (after two hours and thirty minutes, in this case) will they listen and internalize your new ideas or thoughts or proposals. New ideas should not be mentioned until you have successfully completed this fourth stage. The fifth stage is suggesting solutions that will help emotionally and logically to achieve a deeper, more enduring relationship.

Here are twenty-one recommendations I've learned that improve life's experiences and outcomes:

1. *Stay tenacious.* This foregoing episode displayed *tenacity.* Don't let adversity become defeat. Adversity will pass; plan and persevere your way through it to achieve success.

Another note on tenacity—I have had serious asthma my entire life. My attitude toward it is I won't let it slow me down from what I'm going to do, and I will work to understand it better and gradually eliminate it. I surprisingly now think asthma has enhanced my life by giving me more enthusiasm on the days I'm healthy. When I was little and had to watch through the window at the other kids playing outside while I had to stay indoors, it filled me with sadness, eagerness to join in, and great happiness when I could. Each decade, I have diminished my asthma and its impact on me. In my forties, I discovered I had always been allergic to yeast, which was causing much of my asthma (unbeknownst to my doctors). Then when I became vegan in 1997 and gave up dairy, I gained further improvement. I read about possible natural cures and have tried hundreds of things. Although only one or less in a hundred may help, so the odds are long, guess what? I keep researching, experimenting, and pushing forward, knowing that through a series of positive steps, I will succeed.

2. *Be likable.* When people like you, good things come your way.

In business, people want to do deals with our firm because they like and trust our people; this yields opportunities to invest in some of the best companies. Also, as long as you are being genuine, it helps to smile and listen well—that creates mutual bonding. But do this only if it is genuine. You cannot fake affability for long.

When you're well-liked and respected, you can gradually become a leader. Combined with experience and know-how, likeability makes people want you to lead them.

3. *Genuinely care about others.* Show others that you care about them. I really care about other people because I know that each of them is just as important in the universe as I am. Their desires are as important as mine. Their viewpoint is as important as mine. People will view you as likeable and trustworthy when you truly listen to them and genuinely care about them. This will lead to reciprocally beneficial relationships: you will be there for them and they will be there for you. They will want to help you.

4. *Hard work.* Nothing great will be accomplished without a lot of hard work. As a young boy wanting to be a baseball pitcher, I had to learn to throw the ball somewhere near where I was aiming. My wonderful and supportive dad built a wooden frame the size of a batter's strike zone, propped up by a two-by-four angled into the ground behind it. The device was known in Seattle as Old Woody (popularized by a local newspaper). Each time I pitched the ball, trying to get it through the middle of the frame, I had to go fetch the ball. I had to walk a hundred feet to retrieve the ball after each pitch; the ball would

roll up to the garage wall. And if I threw a perfect pitch right down the middle, my reward was that it knocked down the wooden two-by-four propping up old Woody, so I also had to set Woody up again. I spent countless hours practicing throwing a baseball through a wooden frame the size of a batter's strike zone. Eventually, I did become a pretty good pitcher, and it was extremely gratifying.

5. *Live in the other person's shoes.* In your interactions and relationships, if you think about who others are and what their needs and wants are, you will usually be successful in that relationship. People want to be with, and do business with, individuals who value them. Show that by listening carefully, revealing your knowledge of their background and their probable goals, and advising them openly about these and how they could be achieved.

It pays to think about what others will want before a discussion and to prepare responses and solutions in advance by putting yourself in their shoes and imagining what you would want if you were in their situation. After you think about what they want and what their primary motivations are, see if there's a win-win solution available. You can often predict what others will want before a discussion, allowing you to prepare responses and solutions in advance.

6. *Help your counterparts achieve their desires.* Win-win solutions lead to future business opportunities and long-lasting friendships, because people enjoy you and know that you are trustworthy.

7. *Know others.* Know their background, their recent activities, their family, and more. Show genuine interest in them. Talking to others about their family members and remembering their names helps you recognize them as individuals and makes you

more likeable to them. Do some research on individuals before you meet with them. Being genuine and helping others when they're down or suffering (e.g., going to visit them, calling them, or giving some assistance when they're sick, injured, grieving, or otherwise hurting) really deepens relationships.

8. *Speak from the other person's point of view.* For example, say, "I know you want x, and here's how you can get it if we agree to do y and z together." In negotiations, this really disarms the other side's distrust and hostility toward our positions and goals. Also, it helps them to listen better and to consider a broader array of possibilities.

9. *Speak from values.* Speak first from values, not from power or money. Examples of speaking from values would be: "Children will be excited to learn when they come here," or "We're creating the best team," or "Customers will flock to us because of our great service," or "We're going to build the greatest church!" We always tell management, and we mean it, that our first priority is quality. Because our companies are caring for patients, the best outcomes are crucial. Luckily, it's also true that health care providers with the highest quality do better financially as well. This positive association is caused by companies training employees in best practices and measuring continual improvement in results, thereby achieving both quality and financial success.

10. *Listen deeply.* Listen much more than you speak. When listening, search for the speaker's underlying motivations and you will comprehend more deeply.

Notice what topics others choose to talk about, which they seem worried about, and those they avoid discussing. If a person stresses how honest they are, watch out for the opposite. If there are five subjects a person might speak about and they cover only three of them in your conversation, you can know that they are probably not putting enough time, nor are they getting results, in the other two areas, and they are also probably not skilled in those areas.

When speaking to someone about their history, you can learn what type of partner they'll be for you in the future by how they've treated people in the past. I listen for clues when people speak. You can find out what they actually value by prior choices they have made, and you can learn how they will treat subordinates by how they speak about them from the past.

Consciously relaxing while others are speaking helps me listen much better. So does trying to put myself in their shoes: trying to feel what they are saying from their mind and body.

11. *Reputation: your reputation will always precede you.* Always do what you have said you will do. Never say you'll do something if you think there is a chance that you might not. Follow this simple rule, and you will develop a strong reputation that will radiate. People always notice when I always call them at the exact time that I said I would; it shows I value them and their time.

Look for ways to do things that will benefit other people. When I tell someone I will do them a certain favor, or make an introduction, or get some information to them, I do it. I make a written note so I don't forget. These habits make people want to work with you. If I'm not sure I will get something done, I don't say I'll do it; I say, "I'll try to get that for you." That difference is important.

12. *Self-integrity.* Respect yourself and treat yourself the same way reputationally as you treat others. Never promise yourself you'll do something you won't. Do each thing you promise yourself you will do. Your self-worth will grow and grow, and you will become a stronger person.

Here's an unusual example of how to lose respect: years ago as a young man only one year out of graduate school and twenty-nine years old, I was at the closing of a large business deal in New York, a leveraged buyout that we were doing in partnership with the esteemed firm of KKR. The closing table was huge, probably thirty feet long, with documents all over it. One point of contention arose with the lending institution, whose members were also seated at the table. I reminded them that they had already agreed to this point previously, which they vehemently denied. This was a major financial institution that had worked with KKR and our firm in the past. Their president was actually at our transaction's planned signing, and he was denying my assertion.

KKR's partners were quietly watching the action between the lending institution president and myself. I politely told the president that he had sent me a letter that had conceded this point. He denied it, and we were in a disagreeable quandary with everyone, unsure of what to do until he opened his briefcase…that is, when he opened his briefcase and I recognized the top item in it to be the letter I was referring to, and which he had just denied seeing or signing. I immediately pointed to the letter in his briefcase and asked him to reread it. He was aghast at being caught in his lie, and his credibility obviously went to zero. He was caught in a purposeful deceit, and the reputation of his institution and his career suffered irreparably as well.

I make commitments not just to others but to myself as well. If I decide I will exercise tonight, for instance, I do. If I'm not sure I'll work out, I don't commit to myself. I simply tell myself "I might work out tonight." I keep the commitments that I make to myself and endeavor to keep them to others too.

13. *Do your homework.* Do preparation work for each encounter, meeting, email exchange, or call. Review individuals' backgrounds, hobbies, etc. Analyze and know what you want to achieve and how you will arrive there.

Note: when I finished school, I was armed with what I thought were the crucial lessons. But in my first job, I found the single best way to succeed and differentiate myself from others was not a fact from my education, but instead was something I had done consistently throughout my education. The single most important way to succeed was to do homework before each meeting, refresh myself regarding the people involved and the issues to be addressed, and conceive of possible solutions in advance. That's it: just do your homework!

14. *Never burn bridges.* Even when someone wrongs you, speak about their positive attributes. It's a small world, and it's amazing how often that person will later be asked about you when they may be influential regarding an opportunity you want, and how you previously spoke of them will influence whether they say positive things about you.

I'll share with you a remarkable example of how offending anyone could come back to bite you. Several years ago, we had to terminate the CEO of one of our companies. We tried to handle it softly and be friendly and respectful. Over the years, people asked me about that person, and I spoke about his positive attributes and didn't criticize him. (Note that when a CEO doesn't work out, we are partly to blame.)

More recently, we had been working on a transaction for months and had lots of time, money, and sweat invested into the potential deal. I saw the former CEO we had parted ways with, and he told me that he had run into the CEO of the new company we were trying to invest in. Apparently, they knew each other and had lunch together. At that point, I realized how easily he could have hurt us by saying negative things to the CEO of the new company, and he probably could have cost us that opportunity. Instead, he told me that he said very positive things about us and told me how much the new CEO of that company loved us. It was remarkable that he was positive toward us;

he's a big person to do that, and if we had handled his departure any less sensitively, it could have unexpectedly cost us a future transaction.

15. *Family.* Spend extra time with your family members. These are the closest relationships you will have, and they will be the most precious single thing in your life. In our firm, family comes first. Whenever there's an illness or other family issue, we leave work and help or at least visit the ill person. Other teammates can pick up the work we leave behind.

16. *Play as a team. Teams perform better than individuals.* Build teamwork. Act teamwork. Talk teamwork. Teamwork brings the multiple skills of people into one team that is more talented and faster moving than any single person. Each teammate is an extension of the others, doing the right thing at the right time, so the partnership operates as a fast-running machine! A team must be unified in goals and methods, and the best teams build something unique in the world and sell that uniqueness.

Five characteristics of a winning team are:

- Teams must play the game with confidence, and with pride, believing their team *is* the best. And knowing that they each must perform their best *every* day.
- They must have a shared vision that creates uniqueness and generates passion.
- Each teammate must admire every other partner for their talents and forgive their weaknesses.
- Individuals must have different talents. Each is like a facet of a diamond, so the team sparkles in all directions.
- The team must be highly motivated from two sources: from their aspirational vision and from the love of each teammate and positive team spirit!

Team motivation wins!

Good teammates will not exhibit certain behaviors, such as:

- Criticizing the team or teammates.
- Bragging about what they accomplished rather than crediting the team's accomplishment.

Teamwork wins!

17. *Reach for success.* Believe that you can become an amazing star in your chosen area, and when you see a chance, reach for it and take some positive risk.

A Story of Undertaking Some Risk

While in college, I was also working for a conveyor belt company that sold and serviced a variety of conveyor belts used in numerous industries (from cement and wood products production to food services and distribution companies). One afternoon, a call came in from a large timber production and wood products company, Weyerhaeuser Company, and it was urgent. One of their production lines was down due to a broken conveyor belt.

I was the only person available to help them. *There was just one problem*: I had never worked on that particular type of conveyor belt before, and I was somewhat inexperienced. My boss reluctantly dispatched me with a box of tools and pages of written instructions on how to do the repair.

After a lengthy drive, I arrived at the Weyerhaeuser plant and parked in a spot very far from the entrance so I could read the instructions before going in. Just as I grabbed the instructions, a loud noise from my truck's window jarred me. It was a man in Weyerhaeuser coveralls knocking on my window and asking, "Are you here to repair our conveyor belt?" I reluctantly admitted that I was, and he enjoined,

"C'mon, we gotta hurry and get this done! The line is down."

I was in a pickle! I wondered if I should tell him that I'd never repaired this type of belt before so I could freely read the instructions. But then Weyerhaeuser would be exceptionally upset at our company for sending an inexperienced person to fix a vital problem, and I realized they might never do business with our firm again. On the other hand, if I showed confidence and bluffed that I knew how to do this repair, I wouldn't be able to read the instructions, because my new friend was going to stay with me until the job was completed (or, I worried, botched!).

I chose to attempt to save my company's reputation and somehow bluff my way through, but I didn't know how I could make it work. I was very worried and anxious as we made the long walk to the entrance, thinking, "Scotty, beam me up!" As we approached the broken conveyor belt, very fortunately, an idea came to me. I set my toolkit on a workbench about fifteen feet away, and without my new acquaintance seeing, I surreptitiously unfolded the first two pages of the instructions and buried them partway into my toolkit where I could glance at them briefly. Since there were several tools required for the repair (knife, pliers, c- clamps, bonding cement, and more), required for cutting, grinding, measuring, and bonding the belt, I brought only one tool at a time to the belt. I would work on it a bit, then walk back to my toolkit to exchange tools and sneak a glance at the next instruction.

At a couple of points, I needed to pull the booklet out and turn the page and then rebury it, and not being broadly built, I wasn't sure I could obscure Mr. Weyerhaeuser's view, but I apparently succeeded. Half an hour later, as I was continuing my work, he asked me, "How come you change tools so often?" I responded, "It's what you do to get the best repair." I wasn't sure he bought that, but it was the last tough question he asked. He might have been on to me. After an hour, the belt was ready to be glued and heated, so I fastened the vulcanizer (heating apparatus) around it. As the conveyor belt heated for the next thirty minutes, I was not bored. I was praying!

Later, he and I removed the vulcanizer, I trimmed straight the melted edges, and then came the moment of truth: the operators switched on the conveyor to test the ostensibly repaired belt. I was praying even harder. And...it worked! I was incredibly relieved but acted like it was of course expected. Driving away, I reflected on whether I had made the correct decision and concluded I'd made the best but riskiest decision, and I had executed the gambit and repair quite well. And then I exhaled and was able to feel relaxed for the first time in hours.

18. *Have fun!* Life doesn't have to always be serious, and fun is a great reward. It's free and unlimited. And people love you when you're having fun.

I've loved baseball since I can remember. Memories of watching minor league games with my dad on our black-and-white TV, with plenty of static blemishing the picture, warm my heart. And I was happy playing baseball—I loved little league games, and dressing up in my uniform made me incredibly proud and happy; I recall that when I got to wear my uniform to school, I imagined that I was tops and that all the girls were impressed. At age eleven, while I wasn't the best player on the team, I received the award for most inspirational player, which I now attribute to my enthusiasm that I learned from being ill with the severe childhood asthma that often prevented me from playing with other children. When I felt well enough to play, I was the happiest player on the planet.

19. *Compare, don't judge.*
    • Learn who you are and wish to be. Which behaviors fit you? Which don't?

- Compare away, but do not judge yourself. Compare your actions to who you believe you really are and ask yourself, "Is this behavior consistent with who I really am?"
- Know that the more the first two bullet points above overlap, the more consistent with each other they are, and the happier you will be. Your life will become calmer and less stressed, you will feel happier, and your love and connections with others will become deeper.
- When your action fits your self-belief, you will notice a twinge of happiness, more freedom to choose what you do, and more power over actions you decide to take.

20. *Make all choices proactively, not reactively.* When you decide in advance exactly what you're looking for and you find it through searching, you are proacting, and you generally get what you want. When you listen to what others recommend to you and decide whether or not to go with their suggestions, you are reacting, and you will have bad outcomes using this method. I paid a high emotional price to learn this lesson, and it still pains me when I remember it today. My mom had given me her dad's collection of international coins. It was in a little hand-size box, and it had coins from his travels in the U.S. Navy in World War I. My grandad had been in the Asian theater of the war—I remember my grandad mentioning the Philippines, and there were several other countries. Around age eight, I was playing at recess in the schoolyard, and I told of my coins from my grandad. Another student was excited and wanted me to bring them to school. After being badgered by him several times, I did. This student offered to make me a trade, for I don't remember what, and I told him no. But he continued badgering me, and I finally relented and said yes to his deal. I felt bad at the time, and worse afterwards. I've been saddened ever since that I gave in to his pressure and parted

with something meaningful to me. While sad for me, this is an exact example of responding reactively—reacting to what another offers or wishes us to do rather than using the winning behavior, which is proactively deciding exactly what we want and then searching for that until we find it. In this case, I would have been far better off saying, "No, I care about my grandad's coins and will never part with them." But I didn't. That painful lesson has taught me lots about life however—standing up for what I want my life to be and being proactive with my goals, not reactive to what others wish me to do.

21. *Create your good luck.* Because projects I create are often highly successful, people sometimes think, "Bryan is very lucky." And guess what? That's exactly what I think too, and I'm quite grateful. But the key here is not about Bryan; it's about you! I can show you how to become lucky, and how to have good things happen to you too.

The beginning of this magic coming to your life is believing, thinking, and speaking with positivity. Doing those creates good luck! For example, when I approach something I wish to solve, I tell myself and I believe, "I know there's an answer here." That self-commentary and belief leads to most of my solutions. How? First, I persevere more when I know a thing is doable; second, I don't focus any energy wondering if this is doable or not, and that extra energy goes toward creatively finding the solution; third, I tell myself this is easier than I originally thought it might be; and fourth, creativity comes to us when we know for certain that something is doable.

Conversely, negative beliefs, thoughts, and comments can cause bad luck. Every negative thing you say that criticizes, blames, or diminishes another person causes bad luck for you.

For example, I have learned that CEOs who criticize their competitors do not perform well. Their negativism anesthetizes them to the necessity of improving their own company and blocks their ability to think forwardly. I'm currently training myself to interrupt my negative thoughts and stop them—whether they're about a person or current events. That will give me faster forward progress!

We need to see uncertainty as a friendly force of success (see Chapter 16). We need to believe an unexpected occurrence that we might initially think is bad may actually be pointing us toward our solution—and as we change our direction in response to knowing that the so-called bad news is in fact a directional signpost, it aims us toward the best solution, and our efforts succeed!

To create your magical good luck, it's also necessary to carefully choose which projects to make happen. I've found I can only work on two or three projects at a time, or I won't be able to make them happen, so I focus on and prioritize only two or three projects that share three criteria:

> They are virtuous; they will improve the world in
> some way,
> Their success will help many people,
> They are feasible to accomplish.

By being very realistic about the way the world actually works, I must understand whether I am well positioned to lead the project or not.

I don't start projects where I'm not certain of each of these three criteria. We have a limited amount of time on Earth with which to change the world for the better—I don't squander it on things that won't create laudable outcomes! Time is a gift.

HOW I EARNED $2.2 MILLION WRITING A SCHOOL RECOMMENDATION

One morning at my office, I was puzzling over how to handle this: a leader of a portfolio business division was asking me to write a recommendation for his son (whom I'd never met) to Harvard Business School. The easiest way to do this was to speak on the phone with the young man and then write a typical recommendation. But I knew these normal recommendations are not very effective. I thought about it. And I decided to spend time on this and try to do it well. I invited his son Tom to Chicago to visit our offices so we could get to know each other. We had stimulating discussions, and I felt I understood Tom pretty well and believed he would be successful. He was talented and likable. I wrote a more detailed recommendation that included my perceptions of Tom and his characteristics and why I expected him to succeed. I was very gratified, and happy for him and his family, to see him admitted to Harvard Business School. But it turned out there was more.

About five years later, Tom called me and told me he was engaged in buying and improving some medium-sized companies. I invested in a couple and did very well. Then Tom called me and gave me the name of another company he was buying (I'll call it "Champ"). Small world—I had worked one summer during graduate school at a multi-division company that owned Champ at the time, and I had actually performed monthly analyses of how it performed each month (excellently). I believed that this company remained a very good enterprise, and Tom said they could help Champ grow, so I agreed to invest and requested to invest as much as he would let me.

Because Tom had the investors already lined up, and some of them wanted to invest more, there was only a little Tom could to do help me, which he did. I was able to invest $150,000 additional in Champ for a total of $400,000 and became the largest outside investor thanks to Tom. I was extremely lucky—Tom helped this fine company grow faster, and six years later, Champ was sold, returning the investors sixteen times their investment!! The extra $150,000 I was able to invest (probably because I had helped Tom in the past) earned me a gain of $2.25 million! Writing that recommendation surprisingly created a huge gain for me. You never know what the future holds.

How I Began Learning the Lessons

As a little boy, I loved life and challenges. When I was four or five years old, I was at the ocean with my parents, and they were heading back to our campsite a couple hundred feet away. I had a little plastic shovel and asked what the little air holes in the wet sand were, and they told me clams. I told them I would dig one up with my little plastic shovel, and they let me know that clams can dive extremely quickly, so I'd never be able to get one. I was determined to succeed. For a while, they were right. Then to my delight, I got a very small clam. I was extremely proud I had done what they said I couldn't and enthusiastically showed them my clam, and I was quite surprised at their reaction: "Oh it's just a little one—we were talking about a full-sized clam."

Of course, I was very disappointed at their lack of enthusiasm, but I learned an important lesson that has always been with me: sometimes in life, you must be satisfied, and happy, with your accomplishments all alone—without praise from others—and learn to be motivated by your personal praise for yourself. It's been an important understanding for me as I set forth with my own voyage into life.

Breathing was difficult for me as a child. At age six months old, I developed serious asthma and difficult breathing would plague me throughout my childhood. At age three, I remember being carried through a room, apparently at a hospital, and I was scared as my dad handed me to a stranger. I was carried to the operating room for a tracheotomy (slitting my throat and inserting a breathing tube) as the doctors were apparently very worried about my difficult breathing.

Although I was often short of breath, there was a silver lining to my breathing issues. I remember at about age five or six, one sunny afternoon, standing in my bedroom by my window and watching the kids outside in my yard, playing and running and shouting happily. And I vividly remember wishing so hard that I could join them and play.

But I couldn't.

I believe that episode, and others like it, gave me the enthusiasm to love playing when I could, to appreciate health and my ability to run and play when I could, and gave me a zest for life—a keen appreciation of the moments when I could participate fully. And I believe those episodes gave me the love of life I feel today—an appreciation of playing, inventing, competing, and diving enthusiastically into life.

My wonderful dad helped me become an entrepreneur. We had many raspberry bushes in our yard, and when I was six years old, my dad let me and my sister Charlotte pick them and go to neighbors' homes to sell the raspberries. I usually saved my money for a toy I would eventually be able to buy. Then a few years later, he took me to a large Albertson's grocery store, got the manager, and let me talk the manager into buying my raspberries. He said yes, but we needed to deliver them in certain containers which my dad drove fifteen miles to get for me. I was so proud at the delivery to, and payment from, that store manager.

Another love of mine was listening to shortwave radio, whose signal could travel halfway around the world. I climbed sixty-foot-high fir trees in our yard and strung long antenna wires between them so my shortwave radio could receive stronger radio signals. (My parents were obviously very trusting in allowing me to climb those in pursuit of what I loved.) I would listen to a foreign broadcast, mail the foreign radio station a letter, and receive back a letter emblazoned with a picture of their country's flag, confirming I had received their broadcast. I hung those confirmations on my wall and was especially proud of the one I received from Radio Moscow during the Cold War. I recognized the lies and half-truths in Moscow's broadcasts—half-truths such as they had just exceeded the U.S. in cement produced. I noted that the U.S. had moved forward to using more steel in construction and less concrete. That was the era when their leader Khrushchev took his shoe off and pounded it on the table at a United Nations meeting, proclaiming to the U.S., "We will bury you." I recalled that shoe with satisfaction when President Gorbachev later made peace with the world and opened up Russia.

I also had my own Christmas tradition. While my parents bought a nice tree for inside the house, I would go to an inexpensive tree lot and look for a bedraggled little tree, missing most of its limbs, buy it for twenty-five cents, and pick up broken branches off the ground and take them home with me. Then I would wire the broken branches to the tree trunk and make a symmetrical tree which I placed on the walkway to our front door. I felt satisfaction at my inexpensive accomplishment each year.

Bicycling was another thing I loved, and I learned to ride my bike backward, and something surprising to me also: I learned how go forward on level ground, from a stop, without pedaling. How can this be done? Sitting on the bike, if you turn the handlebars quickly left and right, you will be pulled forward with sufficient pace to balance on the bike.

I was home with asthma lots of days, I read lots of books about baseball, and my mom encouraged me to read biographies of famous people. My dad also taught me to play the card game of bridge. In bridge, the bidding system that was standard around the world involved stating how many "tricks" you would win during the card play, which also communicated to your partner generally what type of cards you held. I realized the bidding system everyone was using was quite suboptimal, and I designed a new system that was far more effective and efficient. My parents went on to employ it competitively with great success while I moved on from bridge to other interests.

I always felt excited to do all I could with this one life I'd been given. Later, in college, I felt I could do some great things, but I wasn't sure what. The first two years in college, I mostly partied and wasn't getting top grades. Because I wanted to be able to go to any graduate school I chose, I knew I had to make a radical change. I went to work for a small conveyor belt company.

I worked there for a year, doing menial work and learning to install conveyor belts. Then I returned to school. I think I had grown up. (I chose to work part-time in high school, college, and graduate school, wanting to pay my own way and not be any burden on my wonderful parents.) Once back at college, I received top grades; I continued working part time; and I thought about my future.

I was independent and did not follow the herd. My nature was to find my own pathway and travel it, regardless of the direction others went. In high school, my advanced math teacher told me he assumed I would be getting an engineering degree in college. But I knew that wasn't for me—I wanted personal interaction with others and being involved with people to be an important part of what I did. In college, I chose to be an economics major, which combined analytical and mathematical work with understanding human behavior. Most of my friends in that high school class did get college engineering degrees as the teacher recommended, but I took my own path.

During college, the economics department wanted me to stay and get my PhD in economics, but I understood once again that the suggested path was not for me. I was more interested in exploring and finding something I would be both excited and challenged by.

This will seem silly to you, but here's another time I innovated. In college, my girlfriend just missed the deadline to turn a paper into her professor's office, and she asked that evening if I might get it to his office so it would be there in the morning when the papers would be picked up. I went to the old four-story brick building where the office was and tried the entrance doors, but they were all locked. I walked around the building, seeking entrance. I was rewarded by finding an open ground-level window and saw a large well-lit room with about twenty people scurrying around to produce the college newspaper. It was in a basement with the floor about seven feet down. I decided to take the chance, and knowing I would be apprehended, I saw a wood table and jumped down and loudly landed on it. I looked around at all the people and realized no one had noticed the leap and landing noise, and I thought, "Well, they're definitely going to notice when I jump and land on the floor by them, but I'll try to talk my way out of trouble." I leaped from the table down to the floor with another loud landing. I looked around and was astonished—nobody paid any attention. I carried the papers through the long room and exited to a stairway ascending to the professor's office, where I slid the paper under his door. I then exited via a different route, out the main doors, in disbelief that had happened without me being noticed!

*　　*　　*

I had occasionally read about entrepreneurs building wonderful companies, and I noted that many had gone to Harvard Business School. Believing I wished to do something entrepreneurial, I decided to apply. Then my academic counselor told me that Harvard had a new program where I could also get a Harvard Law School degree, both in four years. I thought a law degree would give me more understanding, whatever I decided to do. I applied.

Realizing that my application had to stand out from the others, I thought of the person reading stacks of applications and what might get their attention. In the essay answers I wrote, I added some humor and a couple humorous events from my life. I understood the risk that the humor might get my application thrown aside, but I felt my application must stand out. Maybe that made the difference, because I was very fortunately admitted to both schools plus the combined four-year program.

I'll admit the first month at Harvard Business School, I occasionally wondered whether I could successfully compete against the many graduates from Harvard College and other Ivy League schools. But I soon learned, luckily, that I could, and I would be fine working part time and paying my own way through grad school which I did, until the spring quarter of my final year, when I decided to have some fun and play softball with my classmates. I borrowed $1,500 from the university and went and played ball. It was a great decision—I loved these springtime ball games with my classmates, whom I would lure away from a lackluster property class to "Play ball!"

I worked to pay my way through grad school, and I was a janitor for the large apartment building we lived in. I enjoyed getting to know the people in the building, and my least favorite part was cleaning dirty, burned ovens when people left. Besides learning how to vacuum and clean windows well, I learned several life lessons:

Seven Life Lessons I Learned as a Janitor

1. As soon as you wash a glass door perfectly clean, someone's going to come along and open it with their greasy palm and leave a smudge. I learned I must accept those things in life, as

they are inevitable, and accept that I made it perfectly clean for a moment. I also learned that I can't control others.

2. You learn a person's personality and values when they move out of their apartment. People who care about others, and respect themselves, leave their apartment clean—they vacuum and clean it.

3. People who leave a dirty apartment don't care about other people and probably don't respect themselves in the sense that this reflects poorly on them.

4. After the first of my three years as janitor, I gained the additional opportunity of showing and renting the apartments. I learned I could make more money in forty minutes renting out an apartment than I made in five hours of cleaning. The lesson I learned was this: If you can get in a position where there's money flying by (in this case, rent payments), you can put up your hand and catch some by being helpful. Lesson: these jobs will pay more.

5. Some tenants are demanding and rude. Being nice to them didn't help. I learned that some people will never change, and the best strategy is to spend very little time with unpleasant, negative people.

6. Some parts of jobs must be done, even though they are very difficult and time-consuming. Sometimes, the oven cleaning I confronted was horrible—some ovens were so burned and dirty that I had to use the foaming cleanser, wait thirty minutes and then scrub inside, and sometimes repeat this process seven times! Otherwise, it wouldn't be clean, and I knew the next renter wanted it spotless, so I continued the cleaning for extra hours. Luckily, not every tenant left it so dirty!

7. People don't like walking on snowy sidewalks, and I learned that on snowy days I had to leave school early and shovel the apartment sidewalks before people returned home from

work—it was an early lesson in the importance of keeping customers happy.

I wasn't sure what I wanted to do after law and business schools until I heard about the young new venture capital industry. I had been looking for a career of helping young companies grow and investing in them, and that's what venture capital firms did. I was excited by the adventure of working with growth companies and investing! Other students went to law firms, and consulting firms, and large companies from business school, and I was the only student to go into venture capital that year. In fact, there were only two venture capital jobs available in the U.S. that year; it was a nascent business in a recessionary time.

In September of 1976, I became part of the venture capital arm of First Chicago (a proud name when I joined; three mergers later, it is now part of JP Morgan Chase). I was excited to actually try this new business I had chosen. The first weeks increased my excitement. I was given books of information about numerous young companies seeking an investment—each forecasting great success for itself. My role was to ascertain which had actual promise and which opportunities should be politely declined.

I learned that the best predictor of future growth was the recent past growth rate, that high gross profit margins hinted at the existence of less competition, and that the capability and experience of management would make or break most companies.

So how did I, as a freshly minted graduate, understand which characteristics foretold a successful management team? I didn't, and I understood that I didn't. Instead, I relied on how well they seemed to be succeeding with their current company, and I looked for very strong company performance. I would gradually learn, from experiences and mistakes, what defines great leaders, CEOs, and managers (which I describe in Chapter 12).

I discarded most opportunities I saw, and when I was somewhat intrigued, I spoke with the company's CEO, trying to understand how the company might be better and different than competitors, how large the potential future market was, and how well the CEO understood his or her enterprise.

I was loving my life as a venture investor and helping companies grow. The possibilities, the challenges of investigating each company to predict its future, partnering to grow each enterprise, and the high investment returns we were producing—these were all things I loved.

During my second year at First Chicago, I created a new way of analyzing whether we were getting a good enough deal for our investments—in other words, whether we were getting sufficient ownership for the risks inherent in each company. I named it "Bang for the Buck" analysis, and it proved novel and useful.

I arrived at that innovation by wondering. First, I wondered how I could better determine whether we were getting a fair deal. Then, I asked myself what characteristics would define how much ownership we should get in exchange for our dollars. Finally, I thought about how those characteristics should be defined and measured.

When I settled on the best ways to do those things, I combined them and had my Bang for the Buck analysis.

My hypothesis was that in leveraged buyouts, there should be a correlation between how junior our money is in the capital structure (i.e., how much debt or senior equity instruments it was junior to, as a proxy for its risk level) and the percentage of company ownership we should receive per $1 million invested. In other words, the most junior equity—the common stock, being at more risk of principal loss—would receive the most ownership per dollar invested, while a preferred stock senior to the common but junior to the debt would receive less ownership per dollar invested, and if there were a senior preferred stock, it would receive even less ownership per dollar, as it carried lower risk of not being repaid.

Now there's no a priori way to establish how much ownership difference there should be between these different equity instruments, so I analyzed it empirically. I took the prior buyouts we had invested in, decided to look at the entire capital structure as vertical strips of dollars, and turned that into percentiles. The first dollar of debt was at the zero percentile, and if the debt were half of the total dollars for the deal, then the last dollar of debt was at the fiftieth percentile. It averaged at the twenty-fifth percentile. The debt however, being most senior, received no equity ownership. The various equity securities were shown vertically according to their seniority relative to each other, and the percentage of the total financing they represented was shown, as was their average percentile.

I made a database of the other buyouts we had invested in and calculated the percentage of ownership received on average in the prior deals for each percentile. If a new potential investment we were considering in convertible preferred stock averaged at the seventy-fifth percentile, I would then compare the percentage of ownership received in prior deals at the seventy-fifth percentile. This would help me negotiate the new deal, because I knew if the financing proposal offered us too little ownership for our money, I would request more; and if needed, I would show a couple prior deals where we received more ownership at the similar seniority percentile. It helped us get the additional ownership we felt we deserved, and, of course, increased our investment returns.

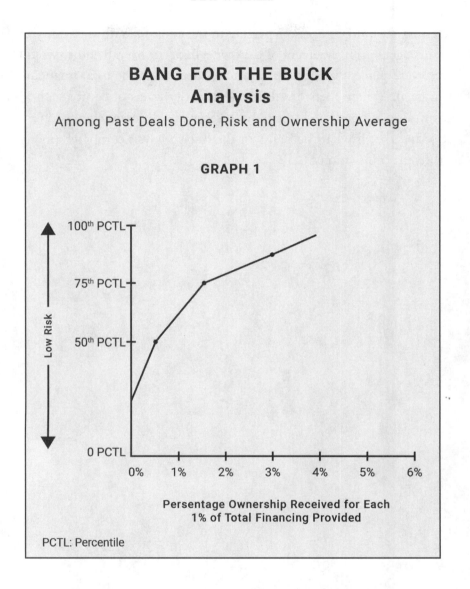

Graph 1. This shows a curve that averaged the risks from a number of prior investments (shown on the vertical axis) with the reward (shown on the horizontal axis). The ownership received is the percentage obtained for each percent of the capital structure invested (capital structure including the debt portion, so that in deal with 50 percent debt and 50 percent equity, an investment of 1 percent of the capital

structure would comprise 2 percent of the equity). With the equity of course getting 100 percent of the ownership, the overall equity would receive 2 percent ownership for each 1 percent of the total financing invested. Where there are different seniority levels of equity such as common and preferred stocks, each receives a different ownership ratio, and that is what the Bang for the Buck analysis compares among different transactions.

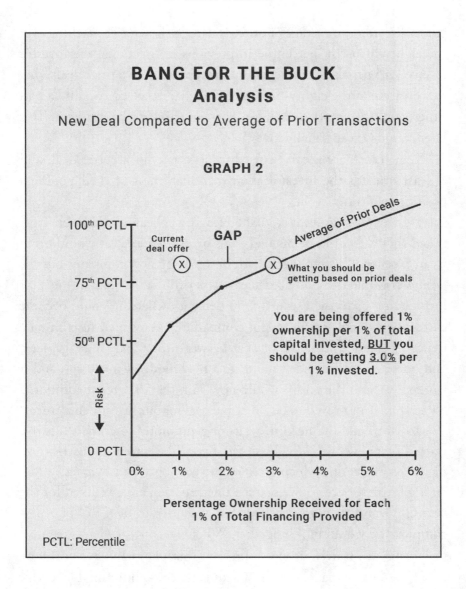

BANG FOR THE BUCK
Analysis

New Deal Compared to Average of Prior Transactions

GRAPH 2

Average of Prior Deals

GAP

Current
deal offer

(X) ⎯⎯⎯⎯ (X) What you should be
getting based on prior deals

You are being offered 1%
ownership per 1% of total
capital invested, <u>BUT</u> you
should be getting <u>3.0%</u> per
1% invested.

100th PCTL

75th PCTL

50th PCTL

↑
Risk
↓

0 PCTL

0%   1%   2%   3%   4%   5%   6%

Persentage Ownership Received for Each
1% of Total Financing Provided

PCTL: Percentile

Graph 2. The curve on Graph 2 shows the average ownership received (the percentage ownership obtained for each 1 percent of the company's total capital structure provided). The X shows that in a particular transaction, the investor is offered 1 percent ownership per each percent invested, at the eighty-fifth percentile of the capital structure as a risk measure. When that offer is compared with the curve showing the average of prior deals, it is shown to be lacking—at the eighty-fifth risk percentile in previous transactions, the investor received 2.5 percent per percent of capital provided. In prior deals, that risk position at the eighty-fifth percentile had received two and a half times as much equity as being offered in this new transaction. This offer sounds exceptionally low!

That information can be used to negotiate for a better deal, and at least informs the investor about reasonableness of their potential position in a transaction.

During my third year at First Chicago, a colleague and I were frustrated that we would be pitched deals by promoters who would bring us an excellent CEO to invest with in starting a new company, but the promoter would demand 50 percent ownership in the company just for introducing us to the executive. 50 percent ownership could become extremely valuable in successful companies! We wanted to eliminate that 50 percent and share all of it between the CEO, management, and ourselves. We decided to create a new mode of investing, and it worked: we and the CEOs would now gain the 50 percent additional ownership. This proved to be a very big deal for our investment returns!

To eliminate the need to wait for a promoter to come to us, we started two new processes. First, we surveyed different industries and niches to determine which areas of the economy and businesses had strong futures. Second, we searched within each area we liked for the best CEO and then approached that executive to be CEO of a new company we would build together. When we convinced an executive to join us, we started a new company; that company created many new locations or made a series of acquisitions—a building-block way of creating an excellent company around a talented management team. The *Wall Street Journal* later recognized us as having invented this new investment process. With this process, we soon started what would become the world's largest paging company, with 10 million customers, and we founded two highly successful cable television companies when that industry was young; later, we created some hospital companies.

In my fourth year, 1980, it was time to leave First Chicago, and I co-founded a new firm, which became Golder Thoma Cressey and Rauner—today called GTCR. The two senior managers in our venture group at First Chicago had decided to leave to start their own firm, and they asked me to join them as one of the three founding partners. I thought about it and realized there was risk in starting a new firm and trying to raise money to invest. However, I saw upsides, like the ability to pay great people adequately so we didn't lose them, the freedom to invest in any good company or industry we liked, doing better economically if we succeeded, and owning our own company. I concluded that with our experience and highly successful investment history, and with the extremely high confidence I had in my two partners, we were likely to succeed.

I vividly remember my little old initial office, with curling square linoleum tiles on the floor, a gray steel desk, cardboard boxes on the floor as my files, and on top of the desk, one old black telephone. And I realized that to climb from these meager beginnings, I would need to use that telephone lots, calling friends, contacts, and companies to create an actual enterprise. I did wonder sometimes, could we go from this meager beginning to success? I thought we could, but a little fear was a helpful motivator!

We had been advised by a partner in another firm that a new firm's first investment was usually a bad one. We tried to be careful and heed that advice, yet the curse befell us too. The first investment we made was in a robotics company, based on my recommendation. It was too early in the robotics industry's development, with too little computing power available for success with robotics. We lost our money.

I have a deep and sad memory of standing with the CEO at that company and telling the seventy employees that the company had failed, and that their jobs were gone. That was so painful to me. It's still a vivid memory, and I knew I never wanted to need to do that again, but instead I wanted to create many, many new jobs.

Luckily, we have been successful at doing just that.

We also made some highly successful investments in that era, including PageNet (our paging company), and Cable Design Technologies, both of which amazingly returned one hundred times our investments. With our collection of investments, including some good ones, a great one, and some losses, we were able to return our investors eleven times their investment in that fund! One sizeable pharmaceutical company took a large gamble on us and invested 10 percent of their entire pension fund with us. Returning eleven times their investment thereby doubled the size of their whole pension fund! I believe our first fund was the best performing fund of any in the early 1980s (and though we've done very well, we haven't quite equaled that eleven-times return since then).

After our first two funds were invested, in 1986, I thought about what it would take to be successful for the next fifteen years. I knew by then that the strategy of focusing more narrowly, and going deeper into the focus area, would win against companies or individuals that invest widely. This approach wins because you have more expertise and experience in your focus area than any generalist could have. There's a kids' card game called war, in which you each turn over one card and the highest number wins; the business strategy we chose of being deeply expert in our area allowed us to turn over the highest card almost every time and win the war.

I reasoned that as our industry became more competitive—as it would, because the existing funds were providing returns well exceeding the stock market—we should focus more tightly and concentrate where we had advantages. I looked back at the investments we had made in our first and second funds, and one thing was quite apparent. Although our overall investment returns were excellent, our investments in early-stage companies—venture deals—had not performed well. In thinking about this, it was further apparent why that would be: many of these companies were developing new technologies, and none of us had technology backgrounds; and there were plenty of firms with strong technology backgrounds on both coasts, especially around

Boston and San Francisco. We were at a competitive disadvantage compared with those firms, and it showed in our venture investments.

However, on the flip side, we were doing amazingly well starting companies in areas we preselected and in which we located an excellent CEO. We also did well with mid-stage growth companies. My partners and I made the decision to cease investing in young technology companies. We would focus where we had competitive advantages and successful experience. That worked exceptionally well for us, and we continued to build good companies and produce strong return through the 1990 and into the 2000s.

By 2002, our industry had become far more competitive. I saw that competition would continue increasing. Once again, I decided that even narrower focus, and deeper knowledge in the focus area, should once again provide competitive advantage, which we needed to regularly produce excellent returns to our investors.

Over my first twenty years in business, I invested in both health care services companies and a number of other businesses including communications and networking products companies. Around 2002, I evaluated the investment returns I had produced in health care deals and in the other areas, and the returns were almost the same—luckily, both were excellent, so the strategic question was not how to get the greater returns, but which strategy would position our team and firm for long-term success.

How did I decide which strategy to employ?

Actually, for several reasons, I thought it was a pretty easy decision. The reasons were that I could see that health care would be a growth area over the long term; health care was a more focused sector in which I had much experience, whereas the other investments I had made were in several fields; and during recessions, health care was relatively stable with some growth, whereas many other sectors suffered declining revenues in downturns.

My partners and I directed all of our attention to investing in health care services. And with increased focus came some great ideas from my brilliant teammates on how we could better identify which health care areas would do well and which might have a tougher next decade. Through the 2000s, our returns remained strong, though not without mistakes—which I sometimes euphemistically call "learning experiences," but which are a very expensive and painful education.

After one millennium ended and another began, the types of companies we were seeking gradually shifted to providing care in the home, and we invested in hospice care (which is the highest patient satisfaction service in all health care); home nursing care; and providing infusions, formerly a hospital-based activity, in patients' homes. Patients love being in their homes.

In 2007, our entire team was excited to join together in creating and building a new health care-focused firm with lofty visions of having a uniquely effective culture, teamwork, and innovative spirit to improve patient outcomes and our health care system, which was riven with wasteful and harmful flaws. Starting the new firm, Cressey and Company, was an arduous but gratifying and inspiring process for all of us. I believe everyone joined enthusiastically in the start-up, because they were inspired by the belief in what our team might create and the health care companies we could help grow.

Today, we have evolved our focusing process, and we make new choices annually about where we will focus our efforts within the numerous health care sectors. And we have additional strategic ideas that will be implemented over the next five years. I've learned that if you want your investment returns to be ahead, your eyes must be fixed on the future. In other words, learn from the past and create the future.

We innovated into conducting activities differently. We improved the way we executed every activity. We also added new value-creating activities to our repertoire and concentrated on the future to create more value.

We recruited exceptionally talented people, who were also kind and caring, and who receive the credit and accolades they greatly deserve. Nobody can do everything incredibly well. Nobody can do everything even regularly well. But those who have some exceptional talents contribute remarkably to team success when they are freed to exercise their talents and other teammates have complementary talents. It's like a beautiful diamond: each facet shines brightly in its own direction, and they join seamlessly with the other facets to create brilliance, beauty, and value.

When teammates do this, you create a championship team that is recognized as the very best.

To improve the way we performed, we assessed each activity as a team to determine does this contribute to our missions: improving the quality of patient health care; growing innovative companies that are moving into the future by improving health care; and creating large investment returns for our investors, who represent pensioners: teachers, police, firemen, and families and life insurance companies.

CONNECTING WITH PEOPLE

The single most important way to achieve the win/win outcomes you desire is *deeply connecting with people*! We can accomplish very little alone; we can accomplish dreams together.

Eight years ago, one of the U.S.'s largest health insurance companies contacted us wanting to meet with us and a portfolio company we had invested in. They were persistent, expressed strong interest, and suggested it would be beneficial for all involved.

We scheduled the meeting in our large conference room, and on a bright, sunlit morning they arrived, with a couple of their senior executives attending. As I shook hands with their most senior person, I noticed that his eye contact with me was quite short, and he quickly averted his gaze to other people. That left me the impression that he didn't care much about me or our firm, or that perhaps he felt squeamish about what they were to propose to us.

They proposed some very unrealistic things at our meeting, more than fair to their company, but very unfair to us and our portfolio company, and parts of their proposals were things we knew they could not and would not deliver. They knew it too but nonetheless tried it out and wasted our time. In hindsight, I realized the senior executive's fleeting eye contact was a tip-off—in this case, that he was bringing disingenuous proposals and that inside himself, he was not comfortable with these.

When meeting people, you can learn lots!

To connect more deeply with people is to succeed more highly. To connect more deeply is to create trust.

Here are things that deepen connection with others.

Because person-to-person engagement is the key to mutual trust, understanding, and mutual accomplishment, do the following:

On important encounters or situations with another person, go one level higher on the engagement scale (see below) than the average person in your position would go.

ENGAGEMENT SCALE

Engagement strength	Communication form
Zero	Silence
Less engagement	Email or voicemail
More engagement	Phone call Video meeting
High engagement	In-person visit
	Prepared* visit

*Preparation work done on the person's background, list of what you want to accomplish, how that will benefit them, where the win-wins are in the mutual opportunity, and what you wish to leave the meeting with as an agreed-upon next step forward.

So, if an average person would send an email, have a phone conversation instead. If the norm would be a phone call, have a video meeting or a personal visit instead. Use the engagement list above, and go further down it toward more engagement to connect more deeply.

At the start of Chapter 4, I related the story of the investment opportunity we had "lost," and how my efforts to restore and deepen connections with those individuals succeeded in allowing a mutually fruitful partnership to be born and flourish. Connection is about the most important thing one can form with others to ensure mutual success through win-win activities, yet most people ignore or pay little attention. The senior health care executive described above squandered an opportunity for a potentially wonderful win-win situation by flouting connection and by not dealing as openly as he might have if he had realized the magic of truly connecting.

Here's how I suggest you begin connecting with another:

GREETING THE OTHER PERSON

The two keys to this are eye contact and a genuine smile. The mistake many people make is to make eye contact too short and to quickly glance at the next person to be met at the meeting or event. Doing that subtly leaves the impression that you're insincere, that you don't care about them.

Watch the length of eye contact the next few times you meet someone. And maintain your eye contact with them a bit longer—you will create a better connection with each other. You're saying they are important to you.

Also, smile! This tells people you're happy to be meeting them and that you'd like to accomplish something with them. When you greet someone, if they don't smile, it can mean that they are not looking for a win-win solution with you—they're looking to win while you lose. Perhaps they don't smile because of the tension they feel anticipating what they expect will be combat that they must win, and perhaps they don't really wish to connect more deeply with you—whichever it is, guard your interests carefully in this situation.

Your goal in connecting deeply is to become more mutually engaged, which builds more trust and allows more mutually beneficial things to be accomplished.

CONNECTING, AND LEARNING, WHEN VISITING PEOPLE AT THEIR COMPANY

A. When you first meet people and have engagingly greeted them, try to find a common interest or sport you both enjoy, similar experiences you've both had, or identify and laud a wonderful person you both know. This *builds trust* and opens up communication, which increases the odds of completing a win-win project together. My experience is that success at this doubles the mutual engagement in the room.

B. Try to find something you can help them or their organization with through something at which you or your company excels. Or perhaps people in your network could help them. Seeking to help gets rewarded in kind.

C. In your conversations, let them know your values, which may be quality, teamwork, integrity, treating people well, or many others. This will deepen their connection with you because they will understand you as a trustworthy person of depth and value.

D. Along with sharing your accomplishments, and your firm's, show your humility: share mistakes you have made and lessons you have learned from those mistakes. The relationship will deepen as you are perceived as more genuine and humble yet capable. And they will view your capabilities as more credible because you are open about your mistakes.

E. If you're trying to sell them on you, be excited about them! Praise the things they have done very well. Specifically note and honor the ways in which they are different and better than other people or firms. And these must be things that are genuinely felt by you—don't try to expand the list by going to things you're not really as impressed with.

F. To ascertain how effective they will be in areas pertinent to you or your company, understand what their strategy is, what they are trying to do that's different than anyone else, and ask yourself if that is a sound idea. Does it fit their strengths? Do they have the resources to accomplish it? If the answers to these three questions are yes, they will probably be successful. If the answer to any of these is no, success is unlikely unless *you* have that missing resource to provide them.

G. Show personal interest in each person you meet at their company, even if they're not a "senior" person. Each person is very important!

H. Have mutual fun at your meeting, meal, or discussion. Don't allow it to become a serious, ponderous visit, but a fun and creative encounter.

CONNECTING ON PHONE CALLS

Your mindset on a call should be confident (thinking that they will be interested in what you have to say), friendly, and engaging. Listen to their tone for the following:

1. Their interest level in speaking with you.
2. Their desired speed for this call (impatient versus relaxed, talkative, and loquacious). Make your speed match their desired speed. This will significantly enhance your odds of a successful call.
3. Listen for what you are interested in and not interested in. Connect on the topic(s) you are interested in and leave the others for later.
4. Introduce subjects that are key to the call from your perspective; in a way, it will make them at least want to listen.
5. If they desire to speak about something else, let them. Only come back to your topic when it seems natural, when you sense they will be engaged enough to listen and consider. You may even be best served by delaying your items to a later call.

BUILD PERMANENT PARTNERSHIPS

In our business, and in most activities, strong relationships tend to come and go. For instance, in our business of investing in growing health care companies, we become very close partners with each CEO, discussing growth ideas, potential acquisitions, financings, employees, and the like; and we speak frequently and also meet in person regularly. We become good friends, navigating through the good times and the difficulties encountered in building companies. And then it's over. We have to sell our investments to cash in our gains, and at that point, we no longer visit or speak regularly. For many people, that's it. They may never speak again, satisfied with a good memory.

That's not how I see things, however. I believe "Once a partner, always a partner." That means I call and speak with them occasionally, and I like to visit them as well. And I always try to ascertain whether there's any ways I can help them, and I also know they will be there to help me. As we talk and meet over the years, our friendship grows deeper, and we know each other better. Whether we may be able to help them in the future or not, our partners know we remain eager to help them, and vice versa. My guiding principle bears repeating: "Once a partner, always a partner."

You have read about some terrific CEOs described in this book, and although we sold our investment in their company, I still consider them close partners, and in fact have flown to see two of them recently whom we ceased legally being investment partners with thirty years ago in one case, and fourteen years ago in the other. We talked about the great things they accomplished, many happy memories, and memories of difficult things we overcame together, too. I will always feel a very close bond; they are my partners.

And they know I am ready to help them if I can anytime they call. You too will benefit from this long-term view of relationships with others.

I care about each person I meet and try to understand them. Knowing that each person is just as important in life as I am, I try to treat them with deep respect. Respect includes listening. Listening to what one says, discerning what they mean, and what their emotions behind their words are. Discerning the emotions behind the words leads to the next step, understanding what their values are. If you gain a sense of the talker's emotions and values, you can accurately understand their personal goals in what they are telling you. And you can ask questions probing their actual goals and motives, to refine your understanding of what you might obtain. When you know what another person is seeking, you can more powerfully create the win-win solution that works!

ACT CONSISTENTLY WITH YOUR BELIEFS

In the late 1990s, we were selling a very successful company that we had helped start along with the talented CEO Tim Burfield. The buyer had offered us a very attractive price, and we were in final negotiations when I received a call from the investment banker representing the buyer. He told me about a provision the buyer must have that would have been detrimental to some of our company's employees. It would have benefitted the buyer somewhat, and I believe the buyer's CEO thought that due to the high price we were receiving, we would give him that term. And I was told the deal was off if we didn't agree to the term.

I recall where I was and what I thought at that moment—I thought to myself that we would not make money on the backs of our employees, so I said no. I was ready to lose the deal over that principle. I heard nothing from the buyer's CEO, and a few days later, the buyer's lawyers were still working on legal documents and the deal moved to completion.

Sometimes it's free to do what's right; sometimes it costs you. But sticking to what you know is right improves your self-worth because you acted consistently with your beliefs.

When working on a potential investment in which we would like the opportunity to buy part of a company and become partners with the management team, I spend much more time thinking about their needs than ours. I try to think creatively about ways they might benefit from a transaction and present those ideas to them. Spending more time assessing and creating benefits to the other side is a key to success.

PRIVATE EQUITY ADVENTURES

Early in my career, we had an investment in Central American hotels, and a group of us went to see them in 1979. The local management team took us on a boat cruise to see the offshore islands near the new hotel, and as we approached a small one, we disembarked to swim and frolic on the shore. The crew rowed us in a smaller launch to the shore. As we walked to the top of the beach to see the interior, our attention was drawn to motion about one hundred feet in front of us—a large, naked man. He and his lady friend seemed shocked, and our crew panicked behind us, yelling to get back to the boat fast—as they ran us to the launch, they said "That's the ambassador. Fast! Back to the boat so he won't know who we are!" The crew seemed more worried than we were as we piled down the sandy beach laughing loudly, jumped into the launch, and headed back to our main boat.

YOUR LIFE MOTTO

At age thirty-eight, I was traveling on a business trip, eating alone one evening in a dimly lit small restaurant in a small town at a Holiday Inn and thinking about my future when I began wondering: "What primary attribute would define me? How did I want to be? What would be noticeably different about me?" I felt the need to establish how I was going to be. What did I aspire to be? It struck me suddenly that I would more fully live out my life's purpose if I had a life motto that I could think of frequently. I recognized that a motto would guide me and accelerate my progress toward what I might become.

I thought for a while about the various things I hoped to do and accomplish with my life, and then I hit upon a short motto that encapsulated what I wanted to be, in everything I did, as I pursued my goals. It was, "Be inspiring." My thinking was, "If I can inspire those around me, their lives will be improved, and together we will accomplish more of our lives' purposes." And also, to be inspiring, I must be inspired, which gives me more energy toward the things I want to accomplish.

"Be inspiring" fit for me, and you can also benefit from sitting quietly sometime, thinking about your life's purpose and the things you wish to do in your future, and create your personal life's motto. Creating it and recalling it frequently will accelerate you toward achieving your dreams!

It's helpful in living your life's purpose (which creates happiness and fulfillment) to establish a short motto for your life.

My motto has magnetically moved me to become what it says by my remembering it frequently—picturing and thinking about being inspiring. When I think of my motto before entering a meeting, I greet others with a little more enthusiasm, I'm a little happier and more confident in what we can accomplish together, a little more interested in getting to know them better, and a little more invested in helping them to achieve their goals. I feel more like the sun is out and the sky is blue.

When I'm living my motto, it positively influences others, and I think it has influenced me to have higher aspirations and to live my core values in everything.

Where my motto has helped

My motto has helped in working with the leaders of companies we invest in. CEOs have said they love working with me, and I think it's because I believe in the great things they can accomplish; also, I care about them and their team, and I give them ideas, possibilities, and the benefit of similar circumstances I have experienced.

To create your own life motto, simply follow the following five steps:

1. Sit and reflect a while about who you are, which words would describe you, in which ways are you different than most other people, ways you're unique, and so forth.

2. Envision what you would like your future life to be like, how you would like to be known in the future, and how you would like to be described by others in the future.

3. Of all the possibilities you have considered, decide which single description you would most like to become in your future.

4. Put that description into a few words. Think about those words as a future description of how you will be known. When you are comfortable with your motto, adopt it as your very own, unique motto. Think of it frequently going forward, and try to remember it at least daily.

5. Watch how you gradually, incessantly become more like your motto, and how you grow into becoming it. Watch eventually as you are described by others in flattering ways reflective of your personal motto.

HAPPINESS THROUGH HELPFULNESS

About five years of age, I was in the back seat of my parents' car, looking up to see out the window and recognizing nothing familiar. "Are we there yet?" I asked. "We're getting there," my mom answered. I knew we were traveling to bring food to a poor family. My mom and dad did this from their desire to help others, and this trip paints a picture I remember. Inside the tiny house we entered, the kids gave me and my sister each a totem pole they had carved and painted. I kept that totem pole, and cherished it, and the memory of our visit with them. The family was excited to receive food and showed their happiness: the kids ran around the small room, the parents laughed with my parents. The family seemed moved, perhaps by experiencing someone caring about them, touched that their own well-being was important to another family and the people in their church.

As a child, my family lived the wisdom that helping others makes us happy and improves our world.

My mother was a trained registered nurse, and I recall walking down our street to see Peggy, whom my mom voluntarily took care of as she was dying from her cancer. At the end of a small pink-painted room was Peggy's six-foot-long bed, right under a triangular window; the sun streamed in on her, and my mom gave her painkiller injections and comforting words of love. I'll never forgot looking and knowing that this very alive person was going to die and be gone from our world. It left a deep impression on me about the reality of death. I still recall the sunlight shining on Peggy on her bed next to the window in her little pink room.

I remember my parents saying yes to welcoming a two-year-old child whose mom could not care for her due to heroin addiction into their home, and whose grandparents asked if my parents might temporarily care for her. "Temporarily" became permanently, and they eventually adopted her, raising her in their home until they were seventy years old; that child, Suzanne, is now my wonderful, loving sister.

My parents were very active in our church—Dad volunteered to preach the sermon at church when our minister was out of town. People loved his sermons, too, because as a family counselor, he certainly understood life, and his messages would connect closely with the audience. He also led the weekly adult education and discussion group for forty-five years! My mom helped lead the women's group of the church and instigated making food, blankets, and other necessities and taking them to the poor.

Mom also drove for Meals on Wheels, delivering to the elderly who could not get or make food. This is a long shot, but I hope that one person whom she helped still lives today, as a single burning candle she lit, with her service remaining in our world today.

When I was seven years old, I remember a special Christmastime when my parents wrapped gifts for kids down the street whose parents were unemployed. My parents told me seriously that I could never let those children know, because these were to be Christmas gifts for them from their parents. And it worked wonderfully—the children received their gifts from several neighborhood families, and nothing was ever said, which was perfect.

Since those times when I was younger, I've learned two important lessons: first, great personal joy and satisfaction develops from helping others—the joy is far different from the happiness that arises from achievement; and second, far greater joy is created by hands-on helping than from giving money. Both acts are wonderful and important to improving our world, but I've obtained far greater joy from personally being directly involved with the individuals as they improve and possibly transform their lives. This produces long-term fulfillment, joy, and happiness.

HOW TO DIAGNOSE ANY COMPANY

How do you know whether a company is worth your time and attention as an employee, as an executive, or as an owner? Remarkably, the factors to evaluate are much the same whether you want to go to work for a new company or you are thinking about investing in it. How would you feel about working at a not-so-great company? Not so excited!

I hope that in understanding this chapter on great companies, you will not only realize how to invest in them, but learn to recognize the dysfunction in mediocre companies and leave if you work there, or avoid putting your money in them if you're investing.

How can you recognize strong companies? Here are the six foundations of outstanding firms:

- Franchise strength

- Human talent and culture
- Growth opportunities
- Value-creation engines
- Processes and information technology advantages
- Operational prowess

These are the foundations of great organizations that can be built further, sometimes rapidly, and that you will want to be a part of—either with your career or with your investments.

I'll explain these one at a time and then describe how to recognize the existence or lack thereof in organizations you see.

Franchise Strength

This means a business's uniqueness and the degree of difficulty other organizations have in competing with the business. For clarity, I'm not speaking here of franchised multilocation enterprises like restaurants, but rather the characteristic of a business that has competitive advantages that allow it higher profitability and growth than other companies who must contend with more substantial competition. A strong franchise advantage may arise from:

1) Brand names like Coca-Cola, Tide, or Belden
2) Patents such as those held by pharmaceutical companies for medicines, which grant exclusivity for a period of time
3) Unique or leading software such as Apple, Microsoft, Google, or Facebook
4) Shelf space in retail stores, like Procter & Gamble maintains with its many successful brands including Crest toothpaste, Bounty, Tide, and Gillette
5) Local service advantages such as those held by leading hospitals or home health care companies like Encompass

6) Advertising that creates strong awareness among consumers such as that used by GEICO and Budweiser
7) Special expertise that is difficult to emulate, such as Warren Buffett's investing capabilities or an artist's talent
8) Technology and engineering capabilities such as those of Google or Apple

Businesses with these strong franchise advantages are harder to compete with, and therefore obtain higher profit margins, volume growth, returns on assets, and benefit from better product expansion opportunities than ordinary competitors.

Human Talent

The second foundation of strong companies is human talent and how it is nurtured and developed. This important subject has several critical elements to consider: leadership, capabilities, team, and culture.

Leadership is the ability to hire and retain highly talented persons, to visualize where the organization should go (i.e., which hill it should take next), and to inspire the team to enthusiastically succeed at its objectives. The leader's communication of purpose, vision, and objectives must be compelling and motivating. It must also create confidence in team members that the team can and will succeed.

A highly entrepreneurial and inspirational leader was Paul Olson, whom I had the great fortune to partner with for fifteen years. Paul brought both leadership and vision. People wanted to follow Paul, and he led them to great places. When we recruited Paul in 1985, we needed a leader of a wire and cable business we had bought, and Paul excited us with his vision of computer networking and the growth possible through pursuing that nascent growth market. First, he recruited some excellent executives with whom he had previously worked. Then, he acquired companies with good products but broken management teams and processes. The first company they bought was Mohawk, a cable producer with a strong history, which was shrinking and laying off employees due to low and declining sales.

Paul Olson's diagnosis?

First, quality problems. Mohawk was shipping products that didn't perform for customers due to poor-quality production. Its reputation was falling like a rock.

The second diagnosed problem was poor customer service. Products that did work weren't shipped on time. Customers could not rely on schedules or on Mohawk's promises. Mohawk was losing money and shrinking when we and Paul Olson bought it. What were the first moves to make? Maximize cash flow by cutting expenses and employees further? Spend more money on advertising and sales? What would you do?

The answer was neither of these. Paul bravely increased the losses initially by first understanding the customers' problems with Mohawk and then tackling and fixing those. Counterintuitively, Paul's first move was to stop shipments (which decreased revenues and increased losses) until each reel of wire had been quality checked, such that only *good* product was being delivered to customers. At the same time, he remade production processes and machinery to produce quality products in the first place. Eventually, less pre-shipment quality inspection would be needed once the factory was producing high-quality products.

After two months of hard work and change at Mohawk, sales gradually started to increase. The losses were becoming smaller. Customers began to trust Mohawk products again.

What was the next key move? Now that quality and customer service issues were resolved, Mohawk needed more revenue to survive. Paul recruited a new sales leader, Mike Degnan. Mike was an enthusiastic, run-through-walls ex-Marine who believed that nothing was impossible. He recruited experienced salespeople who shared the same beliefs. And the next important move? Paul granted some ownership in the company to that sales team and to other key leaders and producers.

Everyone had upside *if* Mohawk became successful. The enthusiasm of the Mohawk team was palpable. The engineering team invented new ways to quickly design custom cable that exactly fit a customer's needs. The sales team traveled widely and espoused the quality and design of Mohawk cable. The production team found needed specialized equipment to ensure quality production.

And what happened? The Mohawk employees became a unified, enthusiastic team. From the factory floor through sales, the enthusiasm to win—and belief they would win—motivated performance. And they had fun. Fun because they were a team, and they were beginning to win as a team. And I think they began to smell a future championship.

Mohawk's sales grew, and it became a profitable growth company. And then the recession hit, and sales became harder to find. What do most companies do at this point? Cut costs and lay off employees? Paul Olson did something entirely different. He adroitly recognized that Mohawk did not have sales coverage across the entire U.S. Instead of hunkering down and cutting costs and waiting for business conditions to improve, Paul did the opposite. He spent more money to grow Mohawk. How? He recruited experienced salespeople into the areas where Mohawk did not have them, and he pushed sales revenue. And Mohawk's sales and earnings grew right through that recession and beyond.

As Mohawk became successful, Paul recruited an accomplished president, George Graeber, and rolled out the rest of his vision. We supported Paul and his team with new money to buy other companies that fit his vision of building a computer networking powerhouse. And they improved the performance of these companies, too, and integrated them into a combined company we named Cable Design Technologies. "Design" connoted customized products, and "Technologies" meant high-speed, leading products.

It was thrilling to watch Paul and his team create a beautiful reality from their visions and dreams. We worked with Cable Design, executing creative financings to allow them to buy companies, improve, and grow; and we worked with the team on their strategy and making acquisitions.

After eight years of fixing and growing, Cable Design Technologies went public with a stock offering on the New York Stock Exchange, and Paul and his team (and I) rang the bell to open trading at the exchange that day. Paul had grown up in the distant town of Duluth, Minnesota, and that day became a leader in New York and internationally.

That was not the end, for Paul continued recruiting great people, motivating them, and buying and integrating companies. After six more years, Cable Design's revenues reached $800 million, having started at only $25 million from our first acquisition fourteen years earlier. The company was a highly respected leader in the networking communications field—and highly profitable. Paul Olson retired in 2000 after an amazing culmination to his remarkable career. We were fortunate to earn an incredible multiple on our original investment we had made in 1985, and many employee shareholders and the public made outstanding gains.

To Cable Design, and to his teammates, Paul Olson brought vision, enthusiasm, creativity, a positive ability to sell, hard work, and a gift of hiring great people and then inspiring and motivating them. And he showed that he was an entrepreneur: Paul did not follow customary prescriptions; he figured out smarter ideas and implemented them.

Team Talent

Every successful team must have a number of and different talents. If all teammates have the same talents, an organization will not thrive. Building to win is analogous to creating a winning football team where many different talents in different-sized people must be found. A football team of eleven large linemen would not succeed, although they could block exceptionally well, nor would one of eleven speedy wide receivers, though they could race down the field. Similarly, a winning business must have numerous complementary talents.

A story of very different but complementary capabilities was our experience with a company that made security systems, alarms, and audio wire. West Penn Wire was started by two very different people. Dave Harden was a creative genius. His unique innovations to make machines run better, and to take inexpensive equipment and modify it to perform high-quality work, were legendary. One time, to use all the production space in a plant, Dave even cut a round hole through a cement wall and had wire being produced on a long, fifty-foot extrusion machine, traveling through that wall to another room, where he placed the other end of the equipment. I fondly remember smiling at Dave's creativity each time I visited and saw the wire being produced through the wall!

Dave's founding partner was an amazing marketing and sales entrepreneur. Don Hastings sold what Dave Harden produced. He devised the creative tactic of selling directly to sound and security system installers, bypassing intermediate distribution. And he developed a catalog for end users, which led to fast growth and rapid adoption.

Don added to West Penn's growth and recognition by hosting and developing the largest party at the annual security installers convention, which grew to unexpected size as attendees clamored to get a ticket to the West Penn party each year. West Penn grew from a two-person start-up to a large national company with multiple plants, many employees, and very happy customers.

And it taught me the value of very different talents: here were two teammates who could not do the other's job, but by combining their unique talents into an unbeatable team, they built a remarkably successful and respected company.

After the talented people are found, the teammates must be motivated to work well together and communicate constantly as they compete with the competitors' teams. Losing organizations allow debilitating internal competition, where individuals seek to look better than their peers, even backbiting and criticizing their teammates. The organization must live and breathe its primary objectives of taking the next hill (e.g., beating the competition in developing the next product, winning important customers, entering a new market). To the extent these laudable goals are minimized in favor of internal rancor, an organization cannot succeed.

Good leaders must eliminate these tendencies by speaking to their vision and removing teammates who cannot give up internal politics in favor of team victories. Removal of these obstructionists is imperative to success. Good team players love team success and count it as personal success when the team wins.

My greatest story of creating an amazing team began with the story of an amazing man, Rocco Ortenzio, a terrific health care enterprise builder who knows how to create a winning team. We have invested in Rocky and his winning teams four times over thirty years. Rocky grew up in a blue-collar, hardworking neighborhood in Harrisburg, Pennsylvania. He worked very hard and was smart, and his desire to help others led him to a professional degree as a physical therapist. That's where his story diverges from the norm. When Rocky began his career, one could quickly see that he was a self-starter and good entrepreneur. After he graduated as a physical therapist, he started a solo practice.

Rocky personally visited physicians to sell them on the idea of referring patients to him. He asked them for just one patient referral so he could show them the caliber of his work. And he left prescription pads with them so they could easily give patients the prescription to visit him. Not surprisingly, Rocky created a very successful practice. But this is just the beginning of the story.

Rocky realized that severely ill or injured patients with large needs for therapy and recovery, such as stroke patients or those recovering from auto and motorcycle accidents, had no specialized facilities to speed their recovery; they were simply placed in normal acute care hospitals or nursing homes. Rocky Ortenzio conceived a better way for the patient: a specialized rehabilitation hospital where patients had physical therapists to work with them, specialized rooms of equipment, and therapeutic-size hot tubs and swimming pools. To facilitate the patients' ability to live at home again, he created mock kitchens so they could relearn being self-sufficient. Rocky invested what money he had, along with money from local physicians that he knew, in the first of these and created a medically successful private rehabilitation hospital in Pennsylvania. After creating the first one and building it into a success, Rocky started the Rehab Hospital Company and ambitiously personally raised $4 million for the subsequent hospital. Then, he grew much further, and the Rehab Hospital Company became a great success.

We met Rocky around that time, when he was building several more rehabilitation hospitals and needed funding to pursue his dream of providing a location for all severely injured patients to have a specialized, healing environment available. Over the next fifteen years, Rocky built the leading company in the field he had envisioned and successfully led it into a growing public company that never lost focus on its theme, making life better, which they constantly did.

I recall speaking, before we invested, with the insurance companies who paid for the services, and they loved Rocky's rehabilitation hospitals, because they saved the system money by healing patients better and faster, returning most of them to their homes rather than to nursing homes. Right then, I knew we would invest.

Rocky delivered an outstanding example of building a great team, even though he began as a solo practitioner. By the time we invested, he had talented leaders in each key role: operations; development of new locations; finance; rehabilitative medicine; and general counsel (his son Bob, who grew to become the extremely capable CEO of the successor company, Select Medical, another highly successful company). Several years later, Rocky taught me another valuable lesson. Although he had performing executives, he recognized that a couple of them could not manage much larger responsibilities, and he proactively upgraded to new executives in those positions. Most leaders wait until there is a problem before upgrading; Rocky showed foresight and leadership by moving before problems developed.

When he decided to sell that company, a good buyer was found, and we stood to make seven times our money invested. On reading the legal documents, I found one term that could expose us to some risk, so I called Rocky and explained it to him. Hilariously (only in hindsight though), Rocky got angry. He said, "Bryan, you should go to church, get down on your knees, and pray and thank God that you have been so lucky here." Years later, when I recounted to Rocky what a searing memory that was for me, he didn't even remember it! Not a memorable moment for Rocky, but a great memory for me!

Another lesson Rocky taught me was to get the business model right first and expand later. He worked diligently on the first several hospitals to get the services optimized, the size right, and to determine the right mix of admitting and attending doctors. Once it was working well, he expanded methodically but quickly, and his company brought America over one hundred new rehabilitation hospitals.

Today, the company has an amazingly talented and complementary team of leaders with different skills—medical, patient quality, acquisition and new location development, operations, human talent leadership, training and education, finance, and a joint venture team to partner with leading U.S. health care systems, which the company regularly does.

Rocky Ortenzio has always had zeal, the desire to make things work better for patients, and the willingness to dive in deeply to make that better way happen, for patients, and for his employees.

Culture: A team's culture manifests the team's values, beliefs, and goals through behavior. Behavior shows in the team's cohesiveness, its positive spirit (or lack of any spirit or presence of dispirit), and the expected outcomes of actions it takes.

Good culture creates good teamwork. Good teamwork creates results that talented individuals working alone could not accomplish. And winning reinforces teamwork and a positive culture.

Culture is the team uniform that binds talented players together in their mission, the shared purpose that motivates them forward enthusiastically. Culture shows the team's cohesiveness and positive spirit.

An outstanding example of great culture generating great performance is Encompass Home Health and Hospice, founded and led by the remarkable April Anthony. Encompass is a home nursing company headquartered in Dallas, Texas, and its culture and founder are discussed further in the next chapter.

How to Build Great Companies

Our firm is very fortunate to have invested with the one home care company that has become widely recognized as the best provider of home nursing to the elderly Medicare patients. Encompass Home Health, inspiringly led by its amazing CEO April Anthony, has created a caring and winning culture. Encompass has an excellent management team, and the culture they have created is energizing its team of twenty-five thousand employees to win with patients, nurses, doctors, and families. Encompass's unique and caring culture is proven by numerous Best Place to Work awards it has earned! No other home nursing company comes close to Encompass.

What does Encompass do that is different? First, they provide their employees continuing education at Encompass University in Dallas, where they bring colleagues to train them further in clinical skills and service to patients. Second, Encompass provides a healthy, caring environment for patients and families, with opportunities for personal advancement. Third, there is a winning atmosphere at Encompass: they strive to be the very best, and that belief is positively contagious. And there's also "Encompass Cares." Employees contribute money and travel on mission trips to help with health care and other services in poorer countries. Employees generate the idea for a service trip and submit their proposal. Chosen proposals provide opportunities to compassionately serve patients while traveling far from home. And closer to home, when a disaster such as a house fire or flood strikes an Encompass family, Encompass Cares is there to rebuild the house and find temporary housing for the affected family. A deeply caring company produces employees who care deeply for their patients and for Encompass.

The culture at Encompass is the best I have ever encountered, and it manifests in employee turnover that is far below industry norms and improves to record levels each year. April Anthony and her exceptional chief operating officer Tracey Kruse visit each location every eighteen months and talk with their colleagues in all three hundred locations in thirty-six states. Dedication to people has created an amazingly positive and caring culture.

That culture has manifested in growth and success. Since we met Encompass, its revenues and earnings have quintupled, it has expanded its service to twenty-seven additional states, and has grown by fifteen thousand new employees.

April Anthony is the only CEO I have known who simultaneously built two different start-up companies into major successes, at the same time! She founded and has served as CEO of two companies for twenty years, and her dedication to, and caring about, her colleagues has created employees dedicated to serving their patients, which in turn has created the company most preferred by patients and their doctors, which has led to growth and success. And it all started with April Anthony and her vision of caring and culture.

A. Growth

Growth is the key to a company's future value. Therefore, it measures the wisdom of investing in, or going to work for a company, today. With growth, and the magic of compounding, a company can ten or twenty years from now be a giant compared to what it is today. Growth companies offer great opportunities. They need numerous enthusiastic, talented people who can succeed and grow with them, and they also need money to support their expansion and new projects; those investments can be amply rewarded.

And larger size allows them to invest in more projects their *customers want. Focusing on customers is the key to succeeding.*

As a company grows, so can its profits and cash flow. Each additional dollar of revenue will contribute more to the bottom line than the previous dollar. How? This is a crucial concept to understanding companies, so make sure you understand the following. A company's expenses should be understood in two categories. The first of these categories is expenses that are incurred each time the company obtains revenue. For example, when a company ships a product to a customer, it costs the company to produce and ship that product, so the cost of material, labor to produce it, and shipping are all incurred for every product sold. These expenses vary directly with the number of products sold, so with that direct connection, these costs are described as "variable costs."

Other costs do not vary when another product is shipped. For example, the people in the offices doing the strategy, product planning, marketing, finance, and accounting exist whether another product is sold or not, as do the office and manufacturing space and equipment.

These costs, our second category, are expressed as fixed costs. Let's take an example: Company A has variable costs of two dollars per each product sold, and the product sells for five dollars. If the company sells one hundred units for $500, and it also has fixed costs of $200, its profit will equal one hundred dollars (after subtracting fixed and total variable costs from the $500 revenue). It has a 20 percent profit margin on those sales. Here comes the magic of growth: if Company A is able to sell one more unit of its product, it receives five dollars and its variable expenses are two dollars, but its *fixed* costs don't change, so it earns three dollars on that additional unit sold, for a 60 percent profit margin on that unit.

Because the incremental sale yields so much profit, it's important to get those additional sales. As a result, successful companies invest in more skilled marketing and sales teams and get their profit margins up. With larger margins, companies can successfully invest in new products or services that their customers want and thereby strengthen relationships with them. Also, these companies will hire more employees to accomplish and execute these growth projects.

One growth story was born right in our offices, when we convinced talented CEO Tim Burfield to build a company with us, and he wished to borrow one of our offices with a desk and a telephone. With no company and no revenue, Tim began making phone calls. His business was institutional pharmacies, which filled and delivered prescriptions to patients in nursing homes. And nursing home patients are large consumers of prescriptions, averaging approximately eight different medications per patient. Tim had been president of another institutional pharmacy company when we lured him away to build a company in his mold, in his vision, with us backing him to accomplish that.

We were excited when he found a good-looking initial acquisition in central Illinois, and we were all deflated when that pharmacy sold to another buyer. But Tim persevered. Over the next several years, Tim made five acquisitions and recruited other talented executives he knew, then strove to impart the best practices performed by any one of those five companies to the other four. I recall attending some of those meetings with pharmacists and managers from all the companies, and I was struck by the enthusiasm and sincerity Tim Burfield exhibited to everyone attending. He wanted to build a great company with great medical services and with people who were improving and improving at what they did. He wanted to help his teammates be the best they could be, and definitely better than the competition.

Tim led American MedServe to a successful public offering, and as the company grew and grew, it was recognized by the largest company in the industry, who made an exceptionally attractive offer for American MedServe, and Tim, ourselves, and the pharmacist-shareholders wished to accept the offer, so we did.

It was an amazing growth story. The company grew organically through great service and improved sales force recruiting, training, and motivation; and it also expanded through acquisitions. In three years, Tim Burfield had led his no-revenue start-up, whose only asset was a borrowed phone and desk, to a value of $250 million, which made the public shareholders, ourselves, and all involved very happy.

How can you find growth companies? First, find industries that are growing. That's easy to research and find online. An average company should grow at its industry growth rate. A good company will grow faster. Secondly, look for companies that have found innovative or improved ways to grow faster. These may include opening new locations, acquiring smaller competitors, introducing new products, or other strategies. For example, Continental Medical, a company in the rehabilitation hospital industry that on average grew about 4 percent per year, opened about eight new hospitals per year in many new markets, and thereby grew approximately 20 percent per year. Midwest Dental, in the dentistry service industry that was growing approximately 2 percent per year, acquired other dental clinics and practices in numerous markets, doing approximately eight acquisitions per year, and thereby expanded about 17 percent annually. An outstanding example of new product innovation is 3M, whose well-known brands include Scotch Tape, Post-it notes, and numerous health care and industrial products. 3M invests 6 percent of its total revenues in research and development, and an impressive 34 percent of its revenue comes from products invented and introduced in the past five years.

Former CEO Inge Thulin said, "For 3M, research and development is the center of [our] plan."

Look to identify superior, innovative companies within growing industries. If these companies have strong business franchises (see prior section on franchise strength), they can continue to succeed for many years.

B. Operations

Many investors underweight a crucial determinant of most companies' success: their operations. The quality of a business's operations touches all phases of the company, and without great operations, success will not be achieved.

Successful companies focus on improving operations and celebrating their operating team's accomplishments frequently. This is a valuable area in which to beat the competition. Effective operations are the foundation of most great companies. This strength allows a company to grow faster, bring more profit to the bottom line, and justify more investment in growth projects than competitors.

Great companies start with great operations.

In our second company with Rocky Ortenzio, a division of the company was performing poorly, and that division had been recently acquired. Rocky created a great example: though he was CEO of a large company with many people at his command, he personally took responsibility, dove in, and lived at that company for six weeks.

He changed the culture, replaced underperforming executives, and quickly had it fixed. Since then, it has been quite profitable.

A lesson in personal responsibility: successful people take personal responsibility for problems and fix them!

Operations excellence.

Here's a list of seven ways great managers display their talent in operations. They show the ability to:

1. Run a business at industry-leading margins
2. Obtain very high customer and employee satisfaction
3. Accurately assess an acquisition's potential and needed changes
4. Effect successful and rapid operational turnarounds
5. Hire "A" position players in needed functions
6. Remove underperformers quickly
7. Produce strong internal growth

Here's a list of lessons learned about choosing companies, which you may use for considering a job or for investing.

C. Lessons Learned for Identifying Companies that Will Succeed:

1. A company can be very profitable if its product or service is only a very small part of its customers' costs.
2. You can see how strong a company's future will be by determining how strong its customers' futures look.
3. High margins are a good quick test of barriers to entry, and a company's franchise value. Look for the ratio of earnings before interest and tax (EBIT), or free cash flow (earnings before interest, tax, depreciation, and amortizations [EBITDA minus maintenance capital expenditures]) to sales of 14 percent or more to find good franchises.
4. Don't join or invest in nongrowth companies; with the wind in your face, it's hard to recover from the inevitable mistakes

or surprises. We could never buy a nongrowth business cheaply enough to make it a happy investment.

5. Ideal companies are a blend of services and products, like medical services plus devices or drugs or supplies. The product portion has leverageable growth and good margins; the service part creates a combination offering that is compelling to customers.

6. A company with good economies of consolidation, that is, high margins from buying and folding in acquisitions, is valuable because you can improve your profit margins by successfully making tuck-in acquisitions.

7. When visiting a company, if the CEO is annoyed that you take notes, check for your wallet and leave fast. They are not planning to do what they're telling you.

8. A company's recent financial numbers tell you what the near future will hold; study the recent trends carefully.

9. A company has no strategy unless it turns down attractive business because it does not fit their strategy.

Targeting for Victory

To know where to concentrate management efforts to realize strong results, first understand what type of company you're in—whether you're in a company that has low franchise value and lower margins—because there, you need to put your efforts and your best resources into finding *efficiencies* which will decrease costs. Conversely, when you're in a high franchise value business with strong margins, you need to focus your efforts and your best resources, on *growth* and improving your service or products for *more growth* and higher revenues.

PRIVATE EQUITY ADVENTURES

One of the hotels we had invested in during the 1970s was located on a hilltop overlooking the town of Tampico, Mexico, known for its silver mines and products. Our company was celebrating a grand opening and invited hundreds of travel agents, restaurateurs, and local VIPs. The party was prepared, and as guests were driving up the winding hillside road to the hotel, the road exploded! It blew up, showering dirt and rocks on arriving cars. Apparently, it had been mined with explosives by a local hotelier utilizing the classic local way of avoiding competition—blowing up their properties! Nobody was injured, but the opening was delayed and occupancy undoubtedly suffered.

Frauds I Have Uncovered

In 1986, I sat at my wooden desk, staring at the wood's grain and pondering the magnitude of what I had just discovered. It was not a positive discovery—I had uncovered a financial fraud! It was incumbent on me to decide what to do with the knowledge and how to handle the situation. This involved a publicly traded company that had been visited by one of my younger colleagues, who assessed it for a potential investment. He returned very excited about this "great opportunity," and he gave me copies of reports by public stock analysts highly recommending purchase of the company's stock.

However, when I later reviewed the company's financial statements, I saw what I now call the Scary Wedge. The wedge is a growing divergence between cash flow and reported profits. I saw that over the past several years, the company's reported profits were steadily and significantly climbing, but the actual cash flowing from their business was negative and rapidly declining. That is unusual, unless a company is heavily investing in future growth projects, such as new locations or research and development. Investing in its future, this company was not! I found the culprit by reviewing their balance sheet; it showed over three hundred days of receivables from customers (this is like not getting paid until eleven months after your services were rendered, which is also eleven months after you have had to pay your employees). A normal company's receivables usually average between forty-five and sixty days. My young associate enthusiastically responded to me,

"Oh, the executives explained that to me. In this business, customers, including insurance companies, pay very slowly, but they always pay!"

I told him, "You can never show me a business with more than three hundred days of receivables without finding that a whole bunch of them will never be collected and should be written off as worthless, and therefore this company hasn't been profitable at all, but it is losing lots of money. And that's what's happening here—look at the cash flow; it's very negative. That negative cash flow shows the real truth here."

My young colleague didn't really accept or like hearing the evidence and conclusion because he was emotional about making a new investment (a bad sign for him as a potential investor); but six months later, the company publicly announced that their board of directors was going to conduct an investigation into the veracity of their financial statements the company had been issuing publicly. Months later, I read that the former CEO had been criminally indicted for defrauding its public investors with false financial statements. I mused with satisfaction that the tools I had used made the fraud obvious to me, far before the company's own auditors or board of directors could detect it. I had decided that the proper action for us to take was to decline to invest, but not to disclose to the company's board of directors that I suspected fraud, because we were able to get information from and visits with companies only on a confidential basis, and we agreed to keep anything we learned confidential. So, we did.

After a year, the company predictably was bankrupt. The lesson I learned about the Scary Wedge would become a valuable tool.

In the 1990s, we were considering a possible investment in another publicly traded company that had been recommended to us by its investment bank with which we were familiar. We took a serious look. For the second time in my career, I saw the Scary Wedge, falling cash flow contrasted to rising reported profits, continuing over several years. So, I asked the investment banker what was going on here, and I astoundingly heard the following:

"Oh, see, what you don't understand is the company keeps three sets of [financial] books: one is for taxes, the second is for public reporting, and the third one is the actual one, and you'll be comfortable with what it shows."

I was shocked, almost stunned, by this outright admission of behavior that sounded quite fraudulent to me. I declined to look any further at the "opportunity." Sure enough, about a year later, I read that the board of directors was investigating the accuracy of the financial statements that the company had been issuing. And in 1993, a court found three of the company's executives and its investment banker were liable for the fraud. The company, of course, was bankrupt.

I was looking to invest some of my personal money in a good stock in 1999, and Enron's stock was all the rage among investors, because it had gone up and up, and it had a creative business model. I decided to review Enron's financial statements to determine whether it looked attractive to me. I remember that moment vividly, sitting in front of the computer in my tower office at home, reviewing Enron, because what I found was very surprising and quite memorable. Guess what I had found again?

Inside the financials of this esteemed, fast-growing company, which had a stock market valuation exceeding $50 billion, I was again looking at the Scary Wedge. Reviewing several years of financial statements on Yahoo Finance, I saw reported profits growing quite rapidly, yet cash flow was very negative. And I recognized two things: this Scary Wedge was the same pattern that had enabled me to identify financial fraud in the two prior public companies where I had discovered it; and Enron *had* to continue selling more stock and borrowing more money from the public (and its employees) just to cover its cash flow losses. It was burning through cash at a huge and alarming rate. I thought to myself, "Unbelievable! Could this be the third public company fraud I've found?" And it was. I was again not surprised a year and a half later when the sad fraud perpetrated on Enron's employees and public shareholders began to unravel and then become totally exposed.

Beware the Scary Wedge! Knowing this pattern may save you lots of hard-earned money someday.

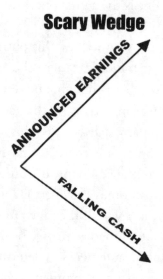

How to Rate a Manager

We learn most about people by observing their behavior when they don't know they're being measured—for example, when we ask direct questions of people, we may get their canned, prepared answer. But when we observe their behavior in specific situations, we can receive important insights into their future performance (see the driving test, the hearing test, the sartorial test, and others in this chapter).

Here are twenty-four ways to rate a manager:

1. Favor people who have succeeded in the past; that's your number-one predictor of future success.

2. Only partner with good horse traders, the type of person you could send out with a broken-down old packhorse in the morning who would return in the afternoon leading a race-horse. Was this CEO a good horse trader? I met a CEO one

afternoon whose company was raising money, and he had a broker named Ernie to assist him. Before the CEO could offer water or coffee at his meeting, Ernie stood up at the conference table, looked down at us, and announced, "You need to know before we start that I get 10 percent of any money you invest." Ernie proceeded to tell us that he would get a board seat on our board of directors, yet he still wasn't done—he would also own 10 percent of the company! And he announced that he had a signed deal with the CEO on those terms. I had never heard of such an outlandish request, so I looked incredulously at the CEO and asked if there was a signed deal for those terms. The CEO sheepishly nodded yes. This CEO didn't even know he'd been robbed, and in our offices, we now refer to an insane request as a "Full Ernie!"

3. Watch the interaction between a leader and the people in their office or plant as you and they walk around. If the manager speaks with and has a good rapport with colleagues, it's a good sign. I once toured a company in Texas where people sitting at rows of desks actually put their heads down when they saw the CEO coming! It was a wave of heads going down in front of us.

4. Bet on likeable people; they have a better chance of being effective leaders.

5. Worriers always win. When we have a CEO who's a worrier, I can sleep well.

6. The hearing test. Beware of the executive who listens too well; he doesn't know what he's doing. I had a CEO when I was young who listened carefully to my thoughts on tactics and said he would try each one. At first, I felt smart; then I thought of a different hypothesis: the CEO didn't know how to operate. Of course, the latter hypothesis was correct. Also beware of the opposite—the executive who doesn't listen at all—he'll drive a company right off the cliff. Ideal CEOs listen carefully but push back on ideas they don't agree with (and use facts and

logic, not emotion, to push back). Great CEOs are willing to admit that others might have a better idea, but I've observed they only implement maybe 30 percent of the external advice they receive, because they do generally know best from their own operating experience.

7. Back the CEO who hires people better than him or herself. Those CEOs succeed and keep the number-one job, because the most important thing a CEO is responsible for is hiring and motivating great people. I once had the experience of attending a first meeting with a growing company, and every time I asked one of the executives a question, their heads would turn to the CEO for permission to answer the query, or allow the CEO to answer it. Obviously, those were very weak teammates, and the CEO would not hire exceptionally good people because he valued being in strict control more than building a highly successful company.

8. A good CEO will talk lots about the company's last six months' performance; a weak one spends most time discussing the future and how great it will be.

9. A good manager cares and talks about earnings (the bottom line)—a weak one talks about revenues.

10. Observe what management teams negotiate for. Offer them trades between current compensation and long-term rewards, like stock. If they're focused exclusively on current compensation, don't invest in them.

11. Managers who negotiate the hardest with you over their deal are typically the best managers. After you make your deal with them, they work on the rest of the world the rest of the time, and you, the investor, benefit.

12. If making acquisitions will be part of the playbook, only back a CEO who has successfully made acquisitions *and* integrated them smoothly and effectively. Those are two different competencies, and both are necessary.

13. Another lesson we've learned is that many CEOs are doomed to failure before they start due to misunderstanding the relationship between the size of their company and its success. Here's the key: a large company should *never* be the goal. *Size is a reward accrued by well-built companies.* Size is an outcome, not an objective. I have visited many young companies where the president bragged about how large they were already, and some even gloated over their various locations evidenced by multicolored pins stuck in a U.S. map on the wall. Their fondest goal was evidently to have large revenue and many locations. I call this the pins in a map syndrome. It's very often a fatal disease to the company infected with it. Why? First, it demonstrates an orientation to the "top line," to revenue, rather than to the "bottom line," or earnings. Earnings constitute a report card on the company's current market position, products or services, and tactical positioning—the top line does not yield these insights.

What happens when a company is overly fascinated with becoming large? In my experience, it expands quickly, without having solved or even defined key portions of its business offering. And when the inevitable problems appear, rather than having to fix them once, the company must endeavor to fix the same problems at many locations. Not only that, but there will be many different problems at different locations.

And if this isn't enough, the company's reputation with its customers is, at this point, horribly tainted, making its success quite unlikely.

Finally, the financial losses associated with these problems may amount to more cash than remains after the company's rapid expansion, leading to bankruptcy. *Don't* buy those multicolored pins for your U.S. map. A business should be proven in the marketplace to be measurably better than the competition before it attempts to be larger than them.

14. When someone claims to have been treated badly by their former employer, check that three times; the opposite is probably the actual story.

15. Watch out for managers that delight in criticizing the competition. Those who bash the competition usually underestimate them. Those who admire, respect, and "good-mouth" the competition stretch farther to improve—and work harder to win—out of perceived necessity and usually succeed.

16. Managers' success comes from striving to provide the best value to customers: the highest quality at the best price, continuously increasing that value.

17. Good managers treat employees as teammates, not subordinates.

18. Avoid CEOs who take the closest parking spot and emblazon their name on it while making other employees park farther away.

19. The CEO's office can be telling. A large, impressive, expensively furnished office is usually pretty, but a very bad sign. Good CEOs invest in their factory and people, *not* in their personal office. The chance of a company's success is inversely correlated to the size of the CEO's office.

20. The sartorial test. Notice how the leader dresses. Managers that are very appearance conscious, i.e., dress very fancy, are usually poor managers. Those who dress just adequately, or nicely, are fine, but the ones who have handkerchiefs hanging out of all their pockets and wear ultra-fancy shoes and excess jewelry are typically poor operators; perhaps they're too concerned with appearances and not enough with the hard work of operating. I once met a CEO who had the reputation of being a turnaround manager; he was dressed exceptionally sharply, he had an accounting background, and I noticed he could indeed improve any company's earnings...in one accounting period!

21. Back people who love other people. They will be loved in return. Back people who are positive.

22. Seek diamonds. A great management team is like a diamond: each facet shines in a different direction. Together, they make a wonderful jewel. To function well, a management team's different skills must complement each other effectively. Most businesses must, at a minimum, have a great operator, an analytical financial person, a visionary, a marketing and sales person, and a great driver of growth.

23. The traditional hierarchy of a business pyramid is actually upside down. The people who make a business succeed are those who touch the customers and those who make the products. They are the top of the pyramid. Management's job is to give them support, freedom, and incentive to succeed. Management can then let these colleagues set their own goals and watch them win.

24. Obtaining the right management team for a company makes all the difference! Great managers know that motivating teammates is not only about financial rewards such as salaries and bonuses, but it is more significantly achieved by inculcating in all colleagues and inspiring them with the mission and values of the company.

Striving together to achieve the company's mission is highly motivational. Most companies' missions are not solely about financial targets but about improving the lives of customers and, in some way, improving the world we live in. Most employees love to be a part of something bigger than they are, such as a mission that will improve the world. This motivates people more strongly than money (in fact, studies have shown that the money employees earn is only the number-three motivator for them), and an effective mission inspires people more strongly, while inspiring positive connections.

Our mission at Cressey and Company follows:

"The mission of Cressey and Company is to cultivate partnerships: build innovative companies, improve America's health care, and create exceptional value and experiences for patients, executive partners, and investors."

Trends as Your Friends

One late morning in 1982, I was visiting a company with Tom Perkins of perhaps the most well-known venture firm in America, Kleiner Perkins. While we were speaking with the company's CEO, Tom received a phone call and told me excitedly after he hung up that one of their biotechnology companies was about to publicly announce a medical breakthrough. That was the early days of biotechnology, which has blossomed and now alleviated or cured many illnesses and holds the promise of major future advances in medicine.

After, I thought about whether I should invest in biotechnology companies. The timing would have been great. However, I concluded that to be a highly successful biotechnology investor, one needed a PhD in biology, chemistry, or a similar field, which I didn't have. I also realized that the growth biotech companies were primarily located around San Francisco and Boston, and I was not. I decided to continue concentrating on areas where I had the knowledge and background to successfully compete.

I've witnessed several tectonic shifts within medicine in my career. In the 1970s, the first for-profit hospital companies were born and were then small; today, they (HCA and Humana) are huge companies succeeding financially and providing quality services. In 1979, I invested in a little system with four small-town hospitals. Although we backed the wrong management team, we were in the right industry, and after changing the management, the company grew highly successfully, ultimately having seventy-one hospitals and billions of dollars in revenues.

In 1984, a small revolution occurred. Hospitals had historically been paid by the Federal government on a cost-plus basis (i.e., the more hospitals spent to provide care, the higher they were paid)! It of course incented inefficiency. Change came that year, when the government began paying hospitals a set amount for each medical condition they treated. A 180-degree turnaround: now, hospitals made more money by spending less per patient treated. Value-based care today continues to spread throughout health care.

In 1986, I could see that it was time for more consumer-convenient health care, and I invested in the new business of surgery centers, where patients could more conveniently have their minor surgeries done than going to the hospital. Surgery centers and the urgent care companies represented the early stages of consumer medicine and retail health care.

In 2005, our firm decided that bringing care to patients' homes would be a growth area for the future, because it's convenient for patients and technology was evolving so that more types of care could be delivered in the home setting. Home nursing was growing, profitable, and highly fragmented; and we recognized that acquiring good clinical organizations and combining them under a great leader— which we fortunately found in April Anthony—could produce better patient care, save money through scale efficiencies, and improve clinical quality.

Since that time, we have also invested in a hospice company, and a company that creates and delivers medically targeted meals to elderly people in their home, plus three information technology companies that have designed software to improve nursing services to homes, and a company providing wound care in the home.

All these trends above that I have experienced in their early stages continue today. The next big trend for health care is, of course, the digitalization of health care: video and telemedicine doctor visits, home telemetry monitoring, artificial intelligence that predicts each home patient's future health state and arranges appropriate care in advance.

Why am I telling you all this? Because much of what you are reading has to do with seeing the world differently and making that a practice. Your own future will be determined in a milieu of increasing change.

Over time, the trends become clear. But from day to day, and particularly when you are just at the beginning of your career, most decisions are not so obvious. What I found, though, is that by asking the right questions and listening carefully, one can find answers that are new and different. One can begin to not only see the future, but create it.

PRIVATE EQUITY ADVENTURES

Once, I was given a spacious three-bedroom hotel suite in Ohio. I awoke during the night and opened my eyes to a small, bright circle moving across the carpet toward me. The light moved closer and was next to my pillow—a spine-tingling awakening for me—I quickly realized there was a robber above me, and I didn't want to be between him and his exit, so I needed to confront and turn him around but without threatening him, so he wouldn't become violent. I decided to say in a sleepy voice, "Rick, is that you?" implying someone else was in the suite with me. I said that without moving, though I prepared for physical action. The flashlight stopped moving, froze on the beige carpet below me, then the intruder yelled "Room service!" and ran through my doorway and down a back staircase to his exit. Phew!

How to Invest Successfully

Wise investing reflects the wonderful fact that humankind continuously improves and invents—improves how it makes products and how it delivers services. Invention is the amazing process of humans dreaming what might be made (the wheel, the airplane, the internet) and ingeniously devising ways to construct amazing new products (and services). These breakthroughs become accepted by the next generation as status quo and become the launching point for another dream. For example, the wheel, which is now used in the guidance systems of spaceships, was originally created in 3400 B.C. in Mesopotamia, where it was used as a pottery wheel. The wheel was used in creating chariots, employed in ancient warfare from about 2000 B.C. until horses superseded the chariot. In China in 231 A.D., the wheel was used to create the wheelbarrow, and it allowed invention of the steam locomotive in Wales in 1804, the invention of the automobile by

Karl Benz in Germany in 1885, and today allows precise guidance in spacecraft.

Humans have improved and improved use of the wheel, exemplifying continuous inventiveness and improvement, which also propels growth in companies and drives stocks' increasing prices. As humankind invents, creates, and devises new ways to make things better, and make new things, each person's productivity increases. New companies are born. Existing companies grow. Witness how the computer has gone from invention by Charles Babbage in the 1830s and development by Alan Turing during WWII to vast computational networks, laptops, the iPhone, artificial intelligence, and has allowed creation of Amazon, Apple, Facebook, Google, IBM, Microsoft, and many more successful companies.

When investing, here are crucial things you need to know that financial firms and advertisements will not tell you:

1. Investing is *not* a way to get rich. Intelligent investing is a way to preserve and grow your money.
2. If you want to get rich, *own* part of the company you work for and help it become highly successful. Or own rental real estate and gradually grow your real estate empire by improving the properties and raising the rents.
3. Or start your own company and make it very successful (See Chapter 3, "Entrepreneurship.").
4. Successful investing requires a long-term philosophy coupled with knowledge of how investing actually works.
5. Investing is *not* short-term trading. In fact, there is an inverse correlation between the frequency of trades an individual investor makes and their returns: the more often one trades, the less money one makes, and the more one may lose.

Short-term trading almost always loses money!

For instance, many people try to become successful "day traders." In fact, over 90 percent of nonprofessional (individual) day traders actually *lose* money (compared to the nicely positive returns I will show you how to make). Therefore, I classify short-term trading as an adrenaline-driven form of gambling, with the odds strongly against you. With investing, the odds are in your favor.

Also, there are numerous professional high-speed trading firms guided by expert mathematicians and utilizing high-speed computers to make numerous small profits on fast and frequent trades. With these powerful firms competing, the individual day trader has a slim chance of winning, but a large chance of losing their money.

Invest in the Unique

Don't be one of numerous copycats.

Early in our firm's history, Steve Jobs and Steve Wozniak had invented the personal computer and started Apple. A different entrepreneur approached us with his design for a personal computer. Since Apple was succeeding (though it was only one thousandth of the size it is today), many companies brought new PCs to market. We invested, and thereby made two mistakes: since there's only room for a handful of companies to succeed in a particular product, our odds of succeeding were terribly low, and the key challenge in this and most businesses was not designing and producing the product; it was getting sales, distribution channels, and advertising so that consumers would know about the product and could buy it. Our company had little knowledge of those things, and even less money to execute them. It failed quickly. I did get one of those PCs and remember learning to use it and thinking that this was one *very expensive* computer, because millions were being lost.

Another lesson I lost money learning was *don't be too early* when investing in something new. In 1985, I led an investment in a health

116

care sector that is huge and growing today, urgent care centers, of which there now ten thousand. We saw the opportunity early, when there were only dozens of urgent care centers in the country. We chose good locations, recruited good physicians, and had excellent facilities. But we failed. We were too early to make money, because at that point, insurance companies did not favor guiding patients to these centers rather than expensive hospital emergency rooms; and patients weren't aware of the alternative of faster, more convenient care because urgent care centers were new and unknown.

Today, many urgent care companies are thriving, but in 1985, we were ten to fifteen years too early. Our vision was right, but our timing was wrong.

Investing in stocks for the long term is wise, because the shares grow in value as the company does. You own actual productive assets managed by creative, talented people.

This crucial linkage allows you to understand the continuously increasing value of stocks over the long run. This increasing value sometimes contrasts with the stock market in the short term, where prices gyrate and markets may fall (or rise) substantially and quickly. But remember: our stock market is gyrating as it rises steadily long-term, driven by our inventiveness and increasing productivity.

Shares of U.S. stocks rise on average 7 percent per year, which means they double about every ten years. Here's some bad news that you should listen to if you decide to invest in stocks:

Emotions can be destructive to one's success investing in the stock market. Emotions are bad news in investing.

Can you resist your emotions in your investing activities? You need to. They'll ruin your results if you don't. Why? Because stock markets occasionally crash and fall significantly around recessions, which are times of fear. During times of fear, humans seek security and safety. And this fear drives people to sell things to maximize their cash holdings. You may hear former shareholders say during a downturn, "We lost half our money in those stocks, but we're selling and at least we'll get half our money back."

And of course, they are selling at the worst time and at the lowest prices, and they lose money. If you cannot resist selling in these circumstances, then do *not* invest in stocks or other long-term assets. Long-term assets will generally produce the best investment returns, but they also fluctuate the most, and you will lose money if you sell during downturns and times of fear.

The same emotional danger also exists at the top of market cycles. When stocks have significantly climbed for some years, and then climb even more rapidly, individuals tend to look at the gains they have made in their stocks and love those gains. The emotional impulse is to buy more, thinking more gains like those can be earned. And shortly after that, the stock market inevitably falls, dashing those dreams and leading to selling again at the bottom. Emotions will lead you to wanting to buy at high prices and to selling very low—an excellent way to lose money.

INVESTING IN PUBLIC MARKETS (STOCKS AND BONDS)

There is a better path available. The U.S. stock market has risen (measured over 150 years) an average of 7 percent per annually. And that single-digit number compounds your money by fifteen times over forty years! Therefore, if you can capture that 7 percent annual return, and you invest steadily through your working years, you will amass a large sum to have in your later years.

To avoid buying stocks at the highs and selling them cheaply, one needs to have a fixed program of investing. It can simply be that you buy a set amount of stock each month or a fixed percentage of your income is used each month to invest.

What stocks to buy?

This is another potential booby trap for investors. The smart thing to do is *not* to try and choose individual stocks. That's gambling, and it will lose you money. Simply buy the Standard and Poor's 500 Index funds (like Vanguard's VFINX Fund, or Fidelity's FUSEX Fund, or similar S&P 500 funds, or the Exchange Traded Fund SPDR S+P 500). This will give you ownership of five hundred of the best companies in America (and they have international operations as well). You will own technology companies, housing enterprises, cellular and social media firms, manufacturing, consumer products, health care companies, and more. You will own a great set of great companies: wonderful coverage of wonderful, growing companies.

A slightly more sophisticated way to invest and manage your portfolio is to preset the percentage of your total investments you wish to have in each asset category, such as stock or bonds. A simple way to invest would be: if you're young, you might invest 80 percent in stocks and 20 percent in bonds. If you are seventy years old with a shorter investment horizon, and wish more certainty of your investment values, you might choose 80 percent bonds and 20 percent stocks.

Bonds

Bonds provide a fixed annual rate of return, and their value fluctuates less than stocks. Returns are lower from bonds than from stocks, but they sometimes rise in value when stocks fall, providing a nice cushion.

I suggest investing in ten-year maturity bonds—longer-term ones can fall more in value when inflation hits and when rates rise, while shorter maturity bonds pay lower interest rates. I would invest one third in safe ten-year U.S. Treasury bonds and two thirds in A-rated U.S. corporate bonds.

Today, this mix of bonds would yield around 2 percent annually, but if rates rise and you are investing regularly, your newer purchases will yield more.

And as the safest asset in your portfolio, this is the one you would sell in case of emergency, as its value will fluctuate less than other asset classes.

Stocks provide the most long-term upside. Making fifteen times your money in forty years at a return of 7 percent annually demonstrates the awesome power of compounding. Even Albert Einstein was impressed with compounding: he said, "Compound interest is the eighth wonder of the world." Another time, he asserted that "the most powerful force in the universe is compound interest."

The most important implication of this is the following:

Do not chase risky or unrealistically high rates of return like 15 or 20 percent, because these usually bring risks of significant losses. You will multiply your money many times just by buying and holding stock index funds. But you can *only* benefit from compounding if you are consistently compounding your money every day, every year. Which means you should not try to time the stock market, guessing when it's low or high, trying to time your purchases. Just make your investment the same day every month, in the same amount, and let compounding over the years make you exceptionally successful. You can only profit from Einstein's eighth wonder of the world if you employ a consistently successful investment strategy, and none has been more proven and consistently successful than the strategy outlined.

In real life, a person is not going to invest at one point and then hold for forty years. A realistic way to invest is to put a set amount monthly into your stock market index fund and to raise that monthly amount as your income increases. And after retirement, you can gradually withdraw money from your account, which should have grown to a sizeable sum of money.

Does this seem too good to be true? Too easy? It is true!

This simple way to invest should earn you large returns, while frequent trading may lose you money. In fact, if you follow this advice, spending little time on investing since you're putting a fixed amount of money into the index fund each month, you will have positive long-run results, while surprisingly, those who give stock investing lots of effort and time and trade frequently usually lose money.

Why doesn't everybody invest this way? Because very few people know these facts and know how markets work. I've told you all you need to know to successfully invest and grow a substantial pot of money in the long term. Alas, some financial firms do not want you investing this way, because they make money selling you different financial products and taking commissions when you trade stocks. They and their brokers may try to lead you in a different direction. You can see many financial and investment ads on television and the internet, seeking to get your business by telling you that investing is very complex, and they know how to do it and you don't. Such firms may benefit from producing many trades in numerous different products. *But you don't benefit!*

And stockbrokers may attempt the same thing in their advertisements: worrying you into thinking you should spend lots of money for them to advise you on your investing. But studies show that these supposedly smart investing services and funds perform much worse on average than the simple method outlined above, and they may even lose you money. Recognize these pleas and exhortations for what they are—an attempt to get your money, not to necessarily show you the best ways to invest.

Do Not *Invest "As Seen on TV."*

Here's some actual advice from recent television commercials:

1) A background voice says that stock indexes were "created for average, and who wants average?" "Firm X will help you aim

for better than average." Sounds good, right? Not if you know the facts, however; if you do, you know this is horrible advice! Why? This firm offers their own mutual funds to invest in, and the problem is that 90 percent of such funds in the U.S. underperform the indexes! Why? Because it's between hard and impossible to consistently beat the stock market averages. Why would these firms spend tens of millions of dollars advertising to us? Because they make money from investors who invest in their funds. And perhaps they don't worry that the investors would almost certainly make more money investing in index funds that mirror the entire stock market's performance.

2) Another commercial features one man asking another why he's so happy. He replies that he's made lots of money this week trading the investments that his brokerage advisor put him into. And he adds that he's been given a perfect portfolio. Sound great? Truthfully, he won't know for years the results of that portfolio, and it is exceptionally likely that it will underperform, as almost all portfolios do, compared with an index fund. You need to understand that stock market averages are *not* the average return received by American investors, which is *far* lower because they invest in the wrong things…that their brokers often put them into because the broker receives commissions and is sometimes more interested in that than the welfare of their client.

PRIVATE COMPANIES AND DEALS FROM FRIENDS

One of your most dangerous investing opportunities will be deals brought to you by "friends." Usually, these are young companies with great dreams. *Do not* invest in these. I did a few times, and what happened to me, I have since learned, is very typical with deals from these sources.

The first "friends' deal" I did was an investment, alongside others in our community, in a small industrial company that was to make acquisitions of other manufacturing companies, improve their operations, and expand earnings.

What actually happened was the following: management proved inept at buying good companies, the operations of the acquired companies actually deteriorated under our "crack management team," and the earnings of purchased companies fell radically instead of improving as was promised. The company's cash flow turned negative: it could not service its debt incurred in making the acquisitions, and we were forced to sell the company with the loss of most of our investment.

So that was a fairly prosaic friends' deal. What about one that promised huge upside and had a large market opportunity? That was the second friends' deal I invested in. The young company was built around a patented blend of chemicals that was "super effective" against bacteria that could be picked up on the skin, by touch. The management and "friend" believed it to be superior to any other product in development and viewed the market potential as enormous, expecting that large consumer products companies such as Procter & Gamble would be interested, that the U.S. government would purchase vast quantities to avoid infections in domestic government agencies, and also that the U.S. military would use the product in its various foreign locations and operations, again purchasing copious quantities.

Hopes were high, but progress was slow. Our company had to fund clinical trials to demonstrate efficacy and assist potential large customers in conducting their own tests.

Delay, delay, and delay.

The hope continued even as the cash waned, and market opportunity continued being described as "huge," but the company needed more money. We investors forwarded more money. The company continued projecting rapidly growing sales but assiduously missed every forecast it made. Significant sales never materialized, so the investors declined to invest more money, and the company ran out of cash and failed.

We lost all of our money on this high-powered dream. What had we missed? Two key things: we had not done sufficient study of the science and evidence around this "miracle" product. It actually did not perform as predicted. Secondly, we paid insufficient attention to the management team's background. They had never brought a new product to market, never sold products to large government agencies, and never conducted clinical trials. Successful companies need management teams that are experienced and proven capable at the key tasks a company will be undertaking. We did not have that and got rinsed in this deal.

Summary?

Do not invest your hard-earned money in friends' private deals. You might as well throw that money in your fireplace—at least it would keep you warm as it disappeared!

There is a saying among investment professionals: "Do you know how to make a small fortune trading stocks and investing in friends' deals? Start with a large fortune."

Fortunately, your own investing life can be winning, and very easy, by ignoring all these "deals," and sticking to the simple method I outlined. You'll do far better and have lots of extra time you might have otherwise wasted trying to understand the world of investing. And you can use the extra time doing things you love.

OTHER TYPES OF INVESTMENTS

You will also be approached to invest in less mainstream assets than stocks and bonds, such as commodities, precious metals, puts and calls, and more.

Don't. These are highly risky, and on average, provide much lower returns. For instance, the most lustrous of precious metals, gold, has produced very dull returns—about 2 percent annually over the last one hundred years, which is close to the average rate of inflation over that period, so in constant purchasing power dollars, there was about zero return. Analysis of other commodities shows similar results. Avoid investing in the assets mentioned above.

What about investing in options, or hedge funds, or private equity or venture capital? Leave these to the pros and stick to stock index funds to maximize your odds of success.

INVESTING LESSONS

1. Diversify your portfolio: have some investments for ultra safety (e.g., shorter-term A-rated bonds) and some for growth (e.g., S&P 500 index funds).

2. Invest only in public stocks or bonds. Don't invest in other people's private companies (unless that's your profession).

3. Don't invest in commodities, futures, or options on stocks (puts, calls, and the like); they are far too volatile and risky.

4. Do not invest in deals that friends or neighbors recommend to you or are involved in. Stick to mainstream alternatives— there are more than enough choices—or invest in your own company.

5. Unless you have an insatiable, uncontrollable urge to be a loser, do *not* buy individual stocks. Even among professional stock pickers, only one in a hundred can consistently beat the market averages long-term. Put the odds on *your* side: buy index funds that track well-known stock indexes such as the S&P 500, Dow Jones, Russell Small Cap, and an international index.

6. Choose an investment allocation mix and stick with it. Avoid the temptation to decrease your target allocation to a particular asset class when it is *down*. Consider decreasing only when an investment type has been *strong*.

7. With bonds, buy a mutual fund that has the maturity (number of years until principle is repaid), risk, and the return characteristics you want. AAA-rated bonds are the highest quality (lowest risk), and therefore pay the least returns. Single-A bonds with a five-to-ten-year maturity are a good basic holding.

8. Tax considerations also matter. Normal bonds are fully taxable. If you are a top-rate taxpayer, consider tax-free municipal bonds ("munies"). High-quality real estate investment trusts (REITs) can also offer good current income and increasing share prices.

9. Gains on stocks or other securities held for more than one year are taxed at only half the normal tax rate (currently 20 percent rather than the 38 percent at the top income bracket). Interest from bonds and REIT distributions are taxed at the higher rate (the 38 percent).

10. Start investing as young as possible. A 6 percent annual return compounds to approximately double in twelve years. But with three times as many years, thirty-six, instead of tripling, your money increases *eight times*! In forty-eight years, it would increase sixteen times. Start investing early and live to a ripe old age; you will be able to afford it.

11. Don't try to "time" the market (investing more when you think it is low, or selling when you think it is high). Markets are random in their movements over short to medium periods of time; no one can accurately predict their direction consistently. Invest evenly over a long period of time, regardless of whether markets have moved your way or against you.

12. Recognize that everyone who gives you advice, and who is with a financial firm, is biased—and is giving you advice that is either slightly or greatly slanted to obtain business and get your money.

13. Do not respond to firms that telephone (hang up quickly) or solicit you by mail (recycle quickly).

14. Do not give the time of day to a self-proclaimed "financial planner," nor a licensed one. Many of them are inexperienced, concerned only about what money they can ease out of your pocket, and not competent to guide you.

15. Never have any personal debt (except a home mortgage—and not that either, once you can afford to be without it). Only buy that (including investments) which you can afford without incurring debt.

16. Investing is a game you win *by not* making the numerous, ordinary mistakes almost everyone else encounters. You don't win by buying a great stock, but by buying and holding an index fund.

Don't fret about choosing the very best investment vehicles. If you follow this plan, your investments will do quite well, primarily because you avoid the insidious crippling mistakes made by most investors.

As the old blessing goes, "May the wind always be at your back."

Private Equity Investing

In 1986, I felt pressure and stress I had not previously experienced. I was faced with two negative options: stop funding expansion of an urgent care company I had helped found only three years earlier, and in effect liquidate it by selling the existing centers to nearby hospitals, or continue funding the losses and probably lose the new investment plus the original one. I agonized over this as I tried to but could not find any good answers.

I had also made an investment in a physician practice management company that treated patients' chronic pain, and I now recognized I had backed the wrong CEO and the doctors' group was challenging to work with. Profits turned to losses, we had to change the CEO, and nothing improved. In fact, the losses increased. Recognizing that I could not fix this, except by investing vast sums and changing the doctors' practice group, which would not be easy, I slowly realized I had lost much of our investment. I was disappointed and worried—worried whether I still had the capability of making the high investment returns I'd been able to produce the prior ten years. I began to doubt myself.

I decided to dig in and analyze these two situations and ascertain what I had missed in analyzing each one. The first thing I realized was that I was very confident going into each transaction, believing that I understood the company's business area quite well. I was chagrined to look back after these investments and realize that I hadn't known their health care areas deeply enough. And I realized that my confidence was totally unwarranted!

I learned I was too confident in my own judgment and had invested in some managers I should not have. I quickly realized, and slowly internalized, that my overconfidence was damaging. This was painful to understand, but not nearly as painful as making bad investments and living with the shame and self-disappointment I felt, and then having to sell the pieces of each company to the appropriate buyer. I vowed to change.

So, on my next investments, I assumed I knew nothing! I asked knowledgeable people about various aspects of the businesses and the health care area. After a while, from those conversations, it would be clear to me whether to make or drop the investment. I learned that I didn't need to personally know everything; I just needed to be humble, assume I knew nothing, and ask smart people who were in that field. Not having to figure everything out actually took a burden off my shoulders. Since then, I've learned that everywhere in life, I have my best results when I'm the humblest. Ego and success are negatively correlated with each other. Decide which you want, success or pride, and if you want success, then you must let go of ego and be humble.

Here are the keys I've learned from forty-plus years of investing private equity in private companies.

The six major items I assess in calibrating the potential success of a company and the size of the potential gains from an investment are:

1. *Industry growth.* Above 6 percent industry growth rate is strong, and the durability of the growth is also important. The likelihood of long-term sustained high growth will allow sale of the company or the investment at a high multiple, because the growth outlook will be strong then too.

2. *Company growth.* For us to invest, the company must grow faster than the industry. We don't want an average company; we want a superior one. A company may exceed its industry growth rate due to its superior business model, faster internal growth due to superior sales and marketing capabilities, a successful acquisition program, or for other reasons.

3. *Business franchise.* It must be robust, which means it's hard for competition to copy or compete with the company—perhaps because it has hard-to-get expertise, economies of scale, or patents and technology.

4. *Management team.* Management should have a proven track record of success in the same or closely related businesses. Having strong individuals in each key functional area is necessary.

5. *Culture.* A strong culture emphasizing teamwork and team success, not individual success, wins. The culture should exude innovation, positivity, and have a virtuous mission at its core.

6. *Business model.* The company's services and products, and how it sells and prices those, as well as the superiority of how it values and serves its customers should lead to high margins and faster growth than companies with differing business models.

But…

Knowing what to look for is great, but how do you find it? And how do you get the opportunity to invest in these outstanding companies? That's what is difficult in private equity investing: finding the opportunity to invest in potentially great companies. Great companies are uncommon, and without the opportunity to invest and partner with them, you will be left with chances to invest in mediocre or highly risky companies, and those abound! Of course, investing in these leads to poor or negative returns.

How Do You Create the Opportunity?

To gain access to potentially excellent companies and investments, a firm (or person) must have a strategy to obtain these opportunities, as well as some characteristics that make the company's management and owners want them as an investor. It may be that a firm or individual specializes in the company's field and knows it well or brings the ability to help increase the company's growth—companies love help with faster growth.

Maybe a firm brings skills that will help the company make positive acquisitions. It can also be that a firm has established a sterling reputation and successful track record, so management teams want to partner with them because of their history.

Given the hurdles to finding and obtaining opportunities to invest in well-positioned private companies, would it make sense to use the private equity measurements like those above to invest in public companies? This might work, but history has proven that almost no investors can exceed the stock market indexes' returns long-term. Private equity firms may produce better returns because they normally have a good enough partnership with management to positively influence the company's growth and value creation, which public stock investors don't get.

Of course, the private equity firm must have the capability: the experience, expertise, people, and know-how to provide value, but a number of private equity firms do have these.

The Three Keys to Major Winners

I define major winners as the investments that return fifteen times the investment or more. It's obviously a high hurdle, but these have major positive impacts on private equity funds' returns.

In reviewing where our firms have produced major winners over the past forty years (and yes, these are still created today), the existence of the following three items appears to allow the creation of a major winner:

1) Huge market so that a major company can be built.
2) Market leader. Building the market-leading company is generally necessary to producing a major winner.
3) Holding the investment a long time, which allows compounding to be your tailwind.

Note that the doable-sounding three times your money in five years is nice, but in ten years, if the fundamentals are sustained, it will be three squared, or nine times; and in fifteen years, it could be three cubed, which is twenty-seven times your money! Long-term sustainability of the company's growth and value creation must be available to reach the major winner level.

In the two companies our firms have been fortunate enough to earn one hundred times our investment in, our value was compounding around five times in five years (38 percent compounded), producing five squared times in ten years, and almost five cubed times (125 times) when we sold (after about fourteen years in both cases).

One Extraordinary Piece of Luck!

I once made an investment where our firm was able to receive eight times our investment in three years *and* increase its ownership in the company! This sounds too good to be true, and it was really good, but it's true and happened in 1988 during our second fund.

Three years after investing, we refinanced a company, and due to its exceptionally strong performance, the company was able to borrow much more money based on its far higher earnings and could pay out ten times investors' original investments. One investor also wished to sell part of their shares, and our firm bought their stock using one-fifth of our potential cash distribution, so we received eight times our money and simultaneously increased our ownership percentage!

And yes, this was one of the companies that earned us one hundred times our investment, so buying that additional stock was a great decision.

THE CREATIVE PROCESS AND THE POWER OF BIG DREAMS

About eight years ago, doctor and former U.S. Senate majority leader Bill Frist was pondering what he might do that would be most helpful to his home state of Tennessee. He came up with improving children's education. Tennessee was ranked forty-eighth, almost the lowest in the nation, and he believed he, with others, could improve that. Most people told Dr. Frist it would be impossible to change. But he was inspired and believed, so he convened a group of school leaders, educators, the teachers' union, and others to tackle the issue. With Dr. Frist as the leader and motivator, over the next seven years, children's educational achievement in Tennessee moved from forty-eighth to twenty-eighth in the nation!

That was an astounding achievement created by one great person who conceived the vision and inspired many others, who enacted the change. Yet it only took about seven hours per week for him! Virtuous power was at work! How could this possibly be achieved?

As I grow in experience, I try to learn more about any natural laws that can provide better ways to see into the future and accomplish objectives more quickly and easily. I'm going to share some things I've found that might be helpful for you in creating important visions and getting your visions achieved!

These are the eight places where powers exist which you can employ:

- Creating visions
- Making your visions happen
- Recognizing uncertainty as your friend
- Leading by inspiring
- Increasing the energy that propels your visions into reality
- Competing more effectively
- Winning more by worrying less
- Actualizing miracles

The steps I'm describing require neither breakthroughs nor mastery; they are force-multiplying powers available to any of us that know how to access them.

CREATING VISIONS

The first idea is visioning. There's great power in a vision that you create and achieve. There are ways we can do this more successfully. A true vision causes people to excitedly give their efforts, creativity, and resources to a project! But how do you create a path breaking vision?

I'll share what I've learned to do, but first I'll define a vision, which I see as a lofty goal that lies between a dream and a strategy.

Strategy sets forth tangible steps toward a visible goal and can describe tactics to be employed. Strategy is firmly grounded in reality. Dreams, contrastingly, are ephemeral. Dreams are airy. They are expressions of things people would love to see come true. And they're usually understood as unlikely to come true if they're detached from reality. We would all love to have a genie pop out of a brass lamp, but that's like waiting for Godot! However, what if you took a dream and attached it to reality? And what if you could envision steps that might achieve that dream and see how it might happen? I call that a vision. A vision is a picture of some great progress, a great accomplishment that most would think is impossible, but which an inspired team could possibly turn into reality.

Many of you probably have several visions, and some may not know how to create a powerful vision. Here's what I've learned about creating visions.

The three primary steps I use follow. First, I describe what the best enterprise in a particular field may look like in ten or twenty years. Or how a charity or business might be far better than what currently exists. In what ways will it be different than today? What will technology allow by then? What would most competitors have trouble copying? Over a period of time, I think about this and make notes on key changes that will take place between today and that future.

The second step I use is creative thinking about what might conceivably happen and what could be manifested. I didn't begin as a creative thinker, but that can be developed! I believe I've learned to think creatively and generate ideas for new possibilities. How? The most important revelation for me was one sentence that one professor at school said in talking about creative people. He said the main difference in creative people is simply that they generate more alternatives, more different ideas when thinking about a problem or when creating something. Since that time, I've generated longer lists of possibilities, even though many are weak, and I've found that sometimes, I hit the best solution late in the list. It helps. The other key to growing your vision is at times when you're having creative thoughts, let those periods continue; make notes of the ideas coming to you and save your notes.

This is a way to channel the ideas your brain and spirit have already created, solutions that you have already subconsciously devised, that most of us never learn to release.

Step three is when I've developed a vision, I don't enact it immediately but let it simmer and morph for months or years until my intuition jumps up and shouts, "It's ready; now's the time! You can go accomplish this." Then, I go into action. I've found that this delay-and-ruminate period seems crucial to getting it right and hitting the ground running.

So why is a vision so important?

A vision propels an enterprise forward. It inspires people and bonds them to their team and their company.

Here's how a vision can deeply inspire:

> A vision that's highly aspirational, that is, contains positive elements of a dream, will strongly appeal to people's emotions; and if it paints a picture of great things, like better lives, wondrous accomplishments, and happier families, it will strongly connect with emotions of care, compassion, love, excitement about the possibilities, and anticipation of great achievements. Powerful emotional connection is the key to obtaining deep commitment and enthusiastic action.

> A vision must also connect to the intellect; it must contain valid ties to reality that make its attainment appear possible. It does not need to be simple. In fact, it should be difficult to inspire deeply. People are more excited about accomplishing something great but difficult than they are something minor but simple.

However, if there is not a logical possible path to attainment of the vision, people will not buy in with their logical thinking.

Inspiration and motivation come from strong emotional and intellectual commitment. Having both types of connection geometrically increases the likelihood of success.

Rocky and Bob Ortenzio have built several amazing companies by creating virtuous visions and building them into powerful enterprises. In Continental Medical, Rocky, who was a physical therapist before becoming a health care maestro, envisioned creating a large rehabilitation hospital company using the best therapies and scale economies to create a health care leader, which he and his son Bob did! Their vision attracted excellent physiatrists and executives who helped build a wonderful company. Their motto was "Making Life Better." Bob and Rocky have since founded and built Select Medical into a successful $7 billion company!

April Anthony built Encompass Home Health and Hospice by envisioning and creating a loving environment that delivers the best care to patients and the best training to caring employees. Talented executives love to be part of her team (and talentless investors can sometimes be lucky enough to join April's team too!).

Making Visions Happen: Virtuous Power

Once you have an important vision you would love your team to attain, how do you turn that vision into reality?

In working to turn visions into reality, I discovered some helpful magic! You can benefit from this discovery. As I better understood what was happening, I named the magic "virtuous power." Virtuous power describes some positive and unexpected things that happen to enable attainment of our visions.

I will explain how virtuous power works in a minute, but first I'll tell you when it is available. Virtuous power is available to help you when first, you have a vision that it is a big one and difficult to attain, and second, your vision is virtuous, so it will help others and would make our world a better place.

Virtuous power helps you attain your vision in four ways.

First, highly talented people from that business or field will come ask to join you! Before you even try to recruit, they are excited by the vision, frustrated by where they've been working, are highly innovative, and want to be part of a breakthrough experience in their field. These people will begin turning your vision into reality.

Second, as you confront large decisions, excellent solutions come to you. At each step of the journey, the successful path will become clear to you.

Third, valuable new ideas will continue coming throughout your journey.

Fourth, as you build toward your vision, other organizations, not just individuals, will join from your community to help you; these substantial relationships will assist your future success.

One example of virtuous power in action is that several years ago, having experienced addiction in my family, and having visited a number of high-reputation residential treatment centers, I recognized that many of them were clinically hollowed out. There was very little effective therapy. And I learned that addiction treatment in the U.S. hadn't changed in eighty years, while all other businesses had vastly improved their models and effectiveness in that time.

I also recognized from my experience that some common-sense, outcome-determining items were missing from all these programs. In response, I decided to create a new type of treatment program, adding those crucial ingredients. And I decided that rather than bringing the new program to the rich, I would bring it to those that would benefit most: the homeless and poor.

The first manifestation of virtuous power for me was being contacted about this by an outstanding business leader and by a nationally known behavioral therapist; they joined and built a highly successful program, with three hundred current patients and eight hundred graduates in just four years. Innovation there is widespread, and we now have a unique and successful program, called Above and Beyond.

I didn't have to expend a whole lot of my time—maybe six hours per week—creating what we have due to the magic of virtuous power, which brought the talented and enthused people who were drawn to the vision. A world expert in addiction treatment has called Above and Beyond's program "a modern treatment miracle in a field badly in need of one."

UNCERTAINTY

Uncertainty, disliked by most people, can allow positive transformation in our lives. We begin to see what reality is once we accept that uncertainty is all around us. To make reality's advantages permanent, we must overcome our distortions. Logically, we may think this pervasive uncertainty can't be right, because it's so different from what we have learned and been taught. We can overcome this by using the new vision and seeing that it produces improved results. We can collect positive data points from the new positive experiences, which begins the logical acceptance of this new tool.

Emotionally, we may resist, due to feeling our old guilt: "I'm not good if I make lots of mistakes," "I'm not responsible for the problems in my life; other people are," "I don't feel like changing; why would I change?" But *do* experiment! There are other emotions, positive ones that will be triggered by positive experiences. You will build confidence and self-esteem as you succeed! And you will experience joy as you accomplish and help others.

The majority of people dislike uncertainty. Most try to avoid it. However, the reality is that uncertainty can become your close friend and your pathway to achievements. I have learned to befriend uncertainty and found many advances by living within it.

Is the following statement true? "People who dislike uncertainty underperform their potential." Yes, it's true.

Thinking about uncertainty should be converted to a series of what-ifs. What if this happens? Then, it should be converted to a set of will-dos! If this happens, we will do these things and gain advantage from the change. And what-ifs should yield some upside ideas on which we can act. Asking specific what-ifs engages your creativity, causing you to identify more possibilities. You will find solutions and better answers as you unleash your inherent creativity on what-if questions. As creatively forming good answers to what-ifs becomes a habit, you will find that most of your best ideas come from this process.

Enacting this, you are living inside uncertainty and creating new possibilities that lead you forward, often rapidly.

Besides inventing new possibilities, you are beginning to see reality. The lenses in front of your eyes are moving, and you are beginning to see more directly forward into your future possibilities. For as you live asking what-if questions, you are acknowledging the many possibilities your future holds, and you are planning your responses to each of them. This becomes seeing reality: while recognizing you can't predict all that will happen, you can be optimally prepared for most of it.

As you learn to work with reality by implementing your what-if answers, you become comfortable with the way our world truly is: uncertain in many respects. Another important benefit is you will worry less, knowing that you have answers to most possibilities and that things will work out well when you operate this way.

Playing the what-if game should yield solutions to existing questions, and uncertainty should cause you to engage in creative thinking, which may yield new directions and new opportunities.

When I decided to create our addiction treatment center, Above and Beyond, I didn't know exactly how I would do it; I had a vision of inventing the treatment program that would gradually replace our ineffective treatment system in the future. And I wanted to bring it to those it would benefit most: the homeless and needy. I had belief it would work, yet I didn't know what each step would be. Whenever I thought, "Bryan, you know this could fail," I logically knew that was possible, but I immediately said to myself, "Banish that thought; Above and Beyond is going to be a great success." Positivity and belief were important here. In January of 2015, I got in my car and drove to Chicago's West Side and began looking at spaces to rent, beginning the search for Above and Beyond's home.

In starting to create this future dream, my head and my heart were aligned, and I was positive about making it happen for all the worthy people who would walk through its doors.

It now graduates about three hundred people a year, helping them save and transform their lives to being loving family members, productive community members, and fulfilled individuals.

In 2020, Above and Beyond was named the nation's top program of the year in the U.S., and also one of America's Best Places to Work! It has become so successful, not because of me, but from the amazing energized people that were attracted to this vision and who are making it reality.

This is a manifestation of the positive powers at work that magnetically attract talented, enthusiastic individuals who want to join the adventure of changing our world to a better one; it's an example of virtuous power at work. All of us have access to these powers, which I believe exist as our toolkit to improve lives, and our world. Take the steps described and the powers will be there to for you to use. I've been amazed at how well the powers work to create good—each of us just needs to create our own virtuous vision and start our own adventurous journey.

As you learn to live in the reality of uncertainty, you will notice some very positive feelings occurring.

First, you will learn that even though most things are uncertain, they will generally develop favorably! When you see reality, you enjoy a better life. With positive experiences, you will develop belief that the future will turn out well. And that does occur more frequently—to your benefit. Gradually, you will experience more comfort and confidence that your life experiences are becoming more positive. You realize you may not know the pathway your life will follow, but you will more frequently love where you arrive and achieve your goals—sometimes via unexpected pathways.

There's a distinction to the realistic uncertainty we can learn to enjoy and live within, which brings comfort that things will work out well; you'll gradually see you don't need to worry because things will be good, and that is different than what most people experience with uncertainty. Most view uncertainty with apprehension or even fear. Most of us want to know what's going to happen and fear it may not be what we wish for. *But* when you learn to let reality work for you, and see it clearly, noticing the upsides of traveling life through the lens of reality, you become more comfortable with your future than ever before. You grow faith in your future, and it becomes more like an adventure, because you realize you don't know all that will happen as you move to your goals. You will worry less than you ever have!

Paul Olson, one of our former CEOs, concentrated continuously on growth opportunities. He didn't have his team construct written long-term plans. Paul was in a cyclical business, and when a recession occurred, Paul didn't cut back; he would invest even more in his growth initiatives, and his company didn't suffer in recessions. He didn't have specific long-term plans. Paul pushed growth, growth, growth. He developed new products, acquired companies, and expanded his sales force. Paul didn't spend much time worrying about downside uncertainty. He was always playing offense. He grew and grew.

Here's another helpful tool I've learned. In meetings with a different company, a banker, or another team, I've learned that when one of them says something that sounds flat wrong, instead of thinking, for example, "Totally wrong," or "They're clueless"—whatever comes to mind—ask yourself instead: what if they're right? What if they know something I don't know? What could it be? If true, what should our team do? And then do homework to discern whether they were right. I've found that about 50 percent of the time I think someone is wrong, it turns out they were right, and their suggestions can yield important understandings that really help us!

Recognizing that I'm often wrong, and seeking the truth instead of seeking to be right, helps me greatly! I'm opening myself to see reality.

The mystery of the unknown can be fun! How? Your people are inspired by your vision, by clarity and passion about your vision. The great things your vision achieves—and the specific ways it changes the future for the better—inspires your team! And the perceived difficulty of climbing that mountain and becoming the best in ways that help others inspires your team too! Understand that your path to those goals will not be a straight one, but it can be a very fun one. As you explore, you *can* figure out what's changing and how to get in front and make that change a tailwind.

Grabbing uncertainty, living inside of uncertainty, discloses your team's future greatness and discloses the pathways that will take your company to the top!

REALITY

Living completely in reality, which most people are unable to do, leads to a life of accomplishments of visions and goals, plus fulfillment in life. Here's why most people can't gain the positive powers reality provides.

Picture yourself seeing through lenses suspended an inch or two in front of each eye. Imagine the lens suspended in front being round and about two inches in diameter. If the lenses are positioned directly in front of your eyes, you see clearly and directly—this corresponds with seeing reality.

However, if the lenses are off to the side, you only see what is sideways, and you're not seeing reality, which is directly confronting you. Most people do not have their lenses in front of their eyes!

For reasons I'll explain, most people do not clearly comprehend the realities of their lives, which also prevents them from directing their lives in highly positive ways. They are driving toward their distant goals on the highway with their eyes shut much of the time, and they're seeing the sideways view instead of the forward scene, so you can understand why their lives feel like they are going sideways, occasionally crashing, and not moving forward.

Negative Barriers

Here's the list of four barriers that prevent many people from seeing reality and impede attainment of the successes they dream of:

1. *Not wanting to admit a mistake.* Especially when young, most of us don't want to raise our hands and acknowledge our mistakes. The biggest problem with that is we don't only hide our mistakes from others, we hide them from ourselves! And we don't learn life's helpful lessons.

   I've learned to admit my mistakes freely; I willingly acknowledge I make mistakes every day—and I learn from them. My life became a lot easier and more successful once I did this.

   One of our CEOs, Tim, would start each board meeting morning by discussing mistakes and problems as if the sky was falling! Then he would say "and here's what we'll do trying to limit the negative impact." When asked whether any progress was showing from those countertactics, he might say, "A little progress." Then, we would hear about more progress, and by the end of the board meeting, I would feel much better. And guess what, Tim had large success with both companies he built, and I'm watching him build a third successful one now. By being a continuous learner and admitting mistakes, Tim built wonderfully successful companies that people loved to work with!

2. *Fear of change.* As humans, habits may save us time and serve us. However, habits not inspected can become ruts. Because change takes effort and creates uncertainty, most people resist even beneficial change.

   I have learned that change often allows a big positive; it's not always the case, but it is true often enough that I now love seeing opportunities where I could change, knowing that is where the upside is.

   I was at dinner one night in Boston with a table of law school classmates twenty years after our graduation. Most of them worked as lawyers, and most of them expressed frustration, such as, "Some of my law clients are getting rich by being entrepreneurs, and I'm smarter than they are—but they're making the big money, not me. It doesn't seem right!" I asked my classmates, "Why don't you do something similar like becoming an entrepreneur and starting or joining a young growth company?" Their responses were, "I'm married and have a home mortgage now," or "I have a family and couldn't take that type of risk."

In other words, in spite of their seeming belief in their capabilities, they were not willing to go for it! They missed the key understanding that the successful entrepreneurs had taken some risks and were willing to encounter uncertainty long before they succeeded.

3. *Ego protection.* Protecting our egos by blocking painful truths about our shortcomings also blinds us to reality, leading us to believe we're steering straight forward as we actually drive sideways. To overcome this, we must consciously remind ourselves, "I don't want to be arrogant or protect my feeling of self-importance—I choose to see the truth and continually succeed."

Our firm once invested in a well-known printing executive who had previously run a large firm, but he was arrogant. We overlooked this and mistakenly invested. Along with arrogance, this leader didn't listen well to ideas from his teammates nor from the directors of his company. Our company that he ran began losing customers and revenues, but he was so insufferably arrogant that his proposed solution was that our investment firm should buy him more companies! We, of course, knew he would wreck those companies too, so we avoided that travesty and fired him. We lost money on that investment, but I learned an enduring lesson and certainly didn't enjoy the education!

4. *Worrying.* Worrying is unpleasant and can lead to fear. People don't want to feel fear, so they don't want to worry. And they

often believe that admitting that reality contains uncertainty will lead them to more worrying, when, in fact, it can diminish worry.

Regularly thinking in obscuring ways moves the lenses in front of your eyes sideways, down, or up. You can't see forward, and you can't accurately see reality. Therefore, you can't effectively deal with reality. Your actions are suboptimal. And worse, you don't hit your goals, which brings disappointment.

How Reality Leads to Success

Seeing reality, the true state of things, allows actions that correspond directly to the truth of situations. I have seen this practice seem to magnetically pull me forward toward my desired outcomes.

When you see reality, you can do something counterintuitive: identifying your weaknesses, which paves your success highway and discloses your magic success levers. And there are many success levers available here. As each team member admits where they are not talented or gifted, the right step to take is to add someone to your team who is gifted in that area. They will move your projects forward, and you will relax, knowing that your weak areas have become great strengths for your team! And you shouldn't spend much time trying to improve your weaknesses, because you can instead hire an all-star in that area. Spend your time using your own gifts and improving on those!

As I've become more experienced, I find more and more things I'm not talented at and view these discoveries as great news, because they allow me to bring in more all-stars to the team, and our achievements and progress build faster.

Seeing reality also allows you to easily focus on a few best actions, and science and business histories prove that those who focus win! Focus leads to becoming the most knowledgeable or best in your focus area, because you delve deepest for great understanding that generalists cannot attain.

Seeing reality also allows you to prioritize well and measure progress, then complete your top few priorities. This accelerates success.

If you complete your top three priorities each year, you will win big. And don't make a loser's move by letting a lesser priority like the tenth on the list take time away from your top three!

Seeing reality allows you to get great people in the important roles required to win.

Seeing reality allows you to more powerfully inspire people as you describe your vision with clarity and passion. People will be further inspired by seeing your team's strong forward momentum.

This combination is unusual, and people love it!

POSITIVE POWERS

More positive powers exist for you to access. Traveling life can be like driving a twelve-cylinder car, but running it with the wrong ignition key, which only fires up two of the twelve cylinders. Here's how you can gain the power of all twelve cylinders and put the wind at your back. The eight keys are:

- Creating your vision
- Seeing reality
- Embracing uncertainty
- Inspiring people
- Creating more energy to attain your vision
- Believing in your success
- Worrying less
- Using the powers (of inspiring, motivating others through mission, motivating through visions of changing the world for the better, creative ideas, miracles arriving, and more)

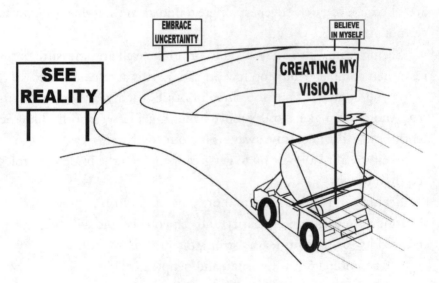

INSPIRING OTHERS

My leadership style is leading not from power and fear, but from inspiration. Here's how I believe inspiring other people works. We most powerfully inspire when we have a vision, and our vision appeals to both emotions and logic.

You'll notice that many sales attempts and leadership efforts use logic and appeal only to the intellect. That may be understood and believed, but it won't inspire action.

Inspiration is what bonds people to their team or their company. When they are deeply excited about and bought into the vision of the firm or the leader, they use their creative efforts and work hard to achieve the mission.

True inspiration comes from strong emotional and intellectual commitment.

With inspirational leadership, it's important to understand these five things that most people want. People want to be:

- Led
- Inspired
- Shown a vision that enthuses them
- Part of doing something amazing and wonderful
- Part of an inspired team

These five things together turn people's humdrum lives into exciting, meaningful adventures. Whether we call it play or work, we enjoy endeavoring together.

Dan Adams started VetCor with a vision of bringing better patient care through creating a more attractive environment for doctors. Great people came to his team, including the COO, who was fortuitously recommended to us by a CEO we had backed in the 1980s. VetCor has become the third-largest and the very best veterinary company in the U.S.

Another example of the magic is Senator Bill Frist deciding to start the first palliative care company. His virtuous vision of improving patients' lives and saving our system money attracted the best geriatricians around the U.S., along with a crackerjack young CEO. With

Dr. Frist's inspiring description of the wonderful things the company would do for patients, he convinced insurance companies to try his palliative care company. Using only a little of his own time, Senator Frist built the company, Aspire, into the industry leader; and five years after he founded the company, it was sold for $440 million! Great people and resources are attracted to virtuous visions!

To inspire emotional connection is crucial, so to further inspire your team, speak to them from values. Don't speak from power, and don't speak from money. Examples of speaking from values could be: "Customers will flock to us because of our great service," or "Children will be excited to learn when they come here."

At Cressey and Company, our first priority is quality, because our companies are caring for patients, and the best outcomes are crucial. Luckily, it's proven that health care providers with the highest quality do best financially too. And quality is a key value that we speak from.

So, make something happen, create your vision, and articulate it succinctly in words that paint a compelling picture, and you'll inspire wonderful people to join you in accomplishing great things!

CREATING MORE ENERGY

My fifth power area is creating more energy for propelling your vision into success, so you can have the future now!

Two ways you can gain more energy to attain your goals surprisingly are forgiveness and suffering; how these work is explained in Chapter 18.

Think about having the *future*…now!

Achieving the vision is not only about having the year 2050 possibilities here now, but it's also having the future spirit and understanding here now! The future spirit is bringing the compassion and love that's possible in the future into your team now.

It's about changing everyone's thinking into seeking great win-wins, not just for them and their teammates, but for other companies and other people too! There's more oxygen in the air when everyone is inhaling win-win! All individuals and all organizations will do better.

COMPETITION

The sixth area of power is competition.

Our firm doesn't compete by trying to step on others and get ahead of them. I don't believe that's the most effective way! We don't compete by elbowing others aside because we're not trying to beat the others; we have bigger goals—we're trying to do things that have never been done!

That takes an entirely different approach. We compete with what we are now, improve to become the best we can possibly be in the future, and then we strive to improve on that.

The goal is to become far better than we would become by simply striving to beat a competitor. We innovate to invent great leaps forward!

WORRYING LESS

Seventh in my areas of power is my positive observation that you succeed more by worrying less.

I say, worry not!

To optimize your success, to achieve your destiny, you will minimize any time spent worrying or wondering about things like, "But what if A doesn't happen?" Worrying takes energy. And it drains energy from the 100 percent you want laser-focused on your future accomplishments. I worry less for two primary reasons:

The first is: when I want something to happen, call it A, I always have a Plan B devised before I learn whether A happened or not. I turn and implement Plan B if A doesn't happen, and I also devise Plan C.

I don't worry, because I know I have another method available that I'm ready to implement. This becomes a habit and leads to comfort with uncertainty.

Not worrying does not mean not thinking—as I described in the "Uncertainty" section, think lots about what-ifs and have counter-measures devised for each negative what-if, but have confidence that your team and company will be highly successful in spite of any speed bumps. Do think about what-ifs, but you don't need to emotionally worry.

You don't know what's best for you! I now realize that I don't know what's best for me. I don't know what should happen next for me to achieve my destiny. Great things can happen after something I didn't want occurred. I've learned to look at the things I wish to happen that don't not as disappointments, but as signs, guardrails, or guides directing me toward where I am supposed to go, toward my best possible destiny. And then great things *do* happen! Once you understand that you don't really know what's best for you, which direction will create the best future for you, then you can relax about what may happen. You can rest assured that life is leading you toward some better future than you had pictured in your mind.

Here's an example. In the sixth month since opening, the homeless addiction treatment center I founded needed a new executive director. We had searched widely and found a person in Montana that seemed decent. One hot afternoon, I received a call from her as she was driving to Chicago to start her new role. She said to me, "Bryan, I'm in my car in Kansas, and I've thought about it and decided not to take the job." I was, of course, crestfallen, as we would need to start our search over.

Then I thought to myself, "Well, this must be good news, and I'll wait to learn why it was good news." Sometimes, I have to wait several years to learn why what happened that I didn't want would prove to have been much better for me. This time, it was only one day.

That night, we received the resumé of Dan Hostetler. He had a remarkable background of success and the right experience for our role. The next morning, I called Dan; he changed his schedule and arrived in my office in thirty minutes. He loved my vision for Above and Beyond, and I loved Dan and his exceptional heart, capabilities, and enthusiasm for Above and Beyond. He has turned out to be better than I could have dreamed: we are now helping far more homeless and poor people beleaguered by addiction, Dan has expanded our unique curriculum, and he has led Above and Beyond to win numerous accolades including a national award, the 2020 Organizational Achievement Award from the National Association of Addiction Professionals, in just its fifth year in existence.

In the end, the bad news was actually amazingly good news! And if you watch, you will see the same things often in your own life and realize that we generally don't know what may be best for the future, so be open to disappointment turning into something grand.

WISDOM WITH EXPERIENCE CAN PRODUCE MAGIC

Here's the eighth and final area of power.

Many people, including executives and other leaders, retire and miss what would have been the most exciting, the most adventurous, the happiest part of their lives! Many young people take a job that doesn't inspire them, yet they stay. And they stay in that rut their entire career. I believe life is meant to progress from becoming skilled at your profession to becoming wise, and then to finding the natural laws that lead to additional powers (like virtuous power, inspiration, insights to help others, spreading love, and more).

I believe these powers are great gifts that can grow forever into what I believe life contains if we believe: a second springtime.

Wisdom and using these powers are life's second springtime. With this comes blossoming, great and unexpected joy can be found in using the new powers that are there awaiting those who learn how to use them.

This discovery of life's great treasures, great experiences, is usually lost by those who remain in a rut. But for those who move forward into what's possible, there is an unexpectedly great adventure—a journey of discovery and joy. This is the chance to become your greatest, and to improve the world and the lives of younger generations.

The magic is there to be used!

Discoveries Await You:
Brainstorming

Brainstorming is an underutilized, highly productive technique that leads to both positive innovation and more excitement and engagement in the team. It is a highly valuable technique that:

- Provides inventive ideas
- Brings colleagues on the outside into topics that are important to achieving the enterprise's mission
- Builds positive teamwork through emotional pleasure via inventing and achieving together
- Creates emotional bonding among teammates

How to Create Great Brainstorming

A leader for the brainstorming session starts by describing the goals of the session (solving a particular problem, creating better ways of achieving a goal, or something else). The group should understand that breakthroughs are the objective, and that there may be multiple improvements (not just one) in a breakthrough, such as accomplishing an outcome more easily or providing better value or satisfaction to customers or fellow teammates.

How do you achieve more than one improvement and create several? You encourage your brainstorming individuals to ask the group what-if questions. Ask what-ifs that are not yet tied to how-tos, but those which posit big new possibilities, suggest different pathways of thinking about changing and improving, or challenge currently accepted ways. Most what-if questions will not lead directly to new solutions, but they will create an innovative atmosphere in which the group will devise better new solutions! Albert Einstein said that, "If at first an idea is not absurd, then there is no hope for it." And also: "Imagination is more important than knowledge."

All in the brainstorming group should feel empowered to, and responsible for, asking questions that move understanding and possibilities to a more advanced or deeper level, thereby helping invent a more wonderful future.

How Do You Manage Dissent?

Some will propose ideas counter to the direction the group is going or will disagree with the group's direction. Although sometimes seeming negative or awkward, these comments often lead toward a better outcome.

To understand alternative opinions or ideas, probe deeper, such as asking "What is behind what you're thinking? Are there experiences you've had that suggest this?" Gain a more thorough understanding of the point. And then have the group discuss these and go through their own experiences. As appropriate, the leader might mention the session's objectives, priorities, and group capabilities so that all can assess the new or dissenting viewpoints and determine whether they might be positive in deepening understanding and creating the ideal plan forward.

Progress which can be proven comes from testing new ideas against *reality*. At the end of the brainstorming session, establish exactly how the ideas are going to be implemented and create a process for their use, which will test those ideas against *reality*. Some of the ideas will perform well and others won't. Next, your team will hold another brainstorming session to improve the things that aren't working well.

Once you have a well-performing process, then you will test that for *interplay* effects (how the components of the system function with the other components of your new process). Some won't mesh together effectively, so you'll modify some to recognize the interplay and achieve your optimal process or ideas.

If it's new ideas rather than processes that you are creating, test each of them in the same ways, against reality and interplay. Then modify the ideas and how to implement them to create your optimal improvement.

NUMBER OF PEOPLE BRAINSTORMING

Usually, the best number of people in a brainstorming group is two to four. You'll want to exclude from the group people who act competitive with other individuals in the group and those who want to take credit for the team's new ideas and progress.

I find that more than four people in a brainstorming session may create less engagement in each person, because it begins feeling more like a meeting. Deep engagement of each person is critical to making real progress.

ONE-ON-ONE BRAINSTORMING

One-on-one with the right person, you can receive new, creative ideas just by speaking with them. With certain folks, you may have conversations that become exciting with mutual discoveries, and it may be that you are communicating, in parallel with your spoken conversation, nonverbally on the same brain frequency, which I've found helps generate brand new ideas that may illuminate productive new paths. These new ideas are not the next logical step in a discussion; they are flashes of insight that seem to come out of the blue to one of you.

One-on-ones with certain people may bring forth important and novel ideas, which then provide great starting points for future group brainstorming sessions.

Brainstorming is almost a secret, because it is much underused and quite powerful. Using brainstorming gives your enterprise powerful advantages, which you will notice after it becomes an ingrained habit with your team.

Traps to Avoid

Victimhood

The victim mentality. Many of us do not wish to take responsibility for the consequences of our actions. When the outcome is not what was desired, many blame other people for bad circumstances. When you do not take responsibility for what happens, you do not learn the lessons that life offers, and it's these lessons that can propel your future success. Victimhood can become a way of thinking that is analogous to hitting your car's brakes in a race.

For example, I once slightly knew a fellow at church, and one day during coffee hour, he asked me if I would loan him fifty dollars, "which I will pay you back shortly." I loaned him the money, and months later, I hadn't heard from the person and was curious whether he was okay, so I called. Here's an example of victim mentality—the first thing I heard was "I can't believe you would call me about that money!" Wow, a permanent victim, and he felt victimized again. The money luckily didn't matter to me, and I actually appreciated knowing this acquaintance's victim mentality so I could save myself future problems by not associating with him.

Many people choose to fail. They do this by choosing "victimhood." They think of themselves as victims, as victims from what happened in their past, as victims from the wrongs done by other people. Victims can't succeed. Why? Because they do not take responsibility for themselves. They don't take responsibility for creating the future they would like. Victims prefer to moan about the unfairness of other people or the pain of their childhood rather than turning forward to create their future. They cannot succeed into their future until they drop the ties to their past and 100 percent let go, looking 100 percent to creating a good future.

Because most of our learning comes from making and admitting mistakes, people in the victim role who don't admit mistakes but simply blame others don't learn, and therefore, they don't succeed.

LIVING THE PAST.

The second trap to avoid, because it could also ruin your life, is failing to let go of past wrongs or suffering. By letting the past go, you increase your energy for creating your future!

I've learned that right now, we should draw a line separating our past from our future and forgive wrongs that were done in the past. Forgiving is not letting wrongdoers in your past off the hook; it's a positive act to benefit yourself! And your future! Think about the past as a rope tied around your waist, and past things that bother you are like anchors twenty feet behind you. As you move forward, it's hard because you're dragging those anchors.

Forgiveness cuts that rope and leaves those anchors behind. You can fly forward! You may not condone what people did in the past, but you give it zero mental energy, knowing the future is all you can change.

It seems counterintuitive, but a source of forward energy is releasing your past suffering.

My father, Charles Cressey, had a challenging childhood, growing up during the depression. He suffered physical abuse from his older siblings and his dad. He wished to become a doctor, but World War II intervened, and since he loved the idea of flying, he became a fighter pilot. Returning from the war, he carried anger about the physical abuse he suffered as a child. At age twenty-two, he thought of his future and reasoned that he could carry that anger the rest of his life, or alternatively, let it go. He decided to let the anger go and live his life with love.

He chose love, and my dad became the first in his family to attend college, then earned a master's degree in social work and became a loving marriage and family counselor who became known for his wisdom, insight, and deep love. I still admire the way he could speak to new acquaintances, listen with keen interest, ask a few questions, and hear their deep issues. People opened up to him. And he shared useful perspective with them. He exuded and expressed love, as he had decided at age twenty-two, and lived a wonderful life. He also taught me much of what I know, and undoubtedly gave me the core of what I now understand.

We have all suffered in the past, and when we bring gratitude and excitement to our lives when the suffering is absent, we create positive energy and enthusiasm!

Cut loose emotional attachment to negative experiences from the past, and you create great energy for your future achievements!

RIGIDITY

The third trap to avoid is rigidity. People who are inflexible can't learn and grow. Whether they are inflexible due to fear of trying anything new or due to arrogance in believing they know the answers to every situation, a rigid person will become disappointed with how her or his life unfolds. Given the importance of making, admitting, and learning from mistakes as the key to future success, those who are inflexible will not develop their creativity in decision-making and living, thereby stunting their development. Nor will they learn from mistakes, which they will want to avoid however possible, so for fear of making mistakes, they will not push themselves to improve, nor will they take the small risks necessary for personal success.

Think flexibly as you live—you will achieve what you want only when you understand the world as it actually is—and you understand that the world constantly changes.

Rigidity loses.

FINDING PURPOSE, JOY, AND FULFILLMENT

I have found joy. Joy that is beyond happiness...a steady, positive glow and feeling. And I didn't find it from the traditional ways of working and succeeding, though they have been rewarding. Those have created happiness, but I've found that happiness peaks and then falls to unhappiness or dissatisfaction, and then rises again. Happiness is good, but it fluctuates and there's something more beyond it.... Something wonderful.

Joy lies beyond happiness. I found joy through realizing that my life's purpose was to help others and to improve my community and our world. I found joy through living my purpose, enacting my purpose. At work, too, living our firm's mission creates joy within me. And watching my teammates enact our mission and improve health care and patients' lives gives me joy. Joy is a constant; it can always be with you, and its presence is grown and nourished through helping others.

A key to creating fulfillment and joy inside you is to love yourself. Remember that each of us is a small speck in the vast universe: as you feel small standing at the ocean's edge, or hiking in forests or mountains, recognize that although you are a speck in the universe, your life is very important to you, and also that everyone else on earth feels the importance of their own life. Understand that every person you see in life is as important to the universe as you are.

Learn that serving others, whether friends or persons in need, increases your own happiness and also makes the world a better place. This is a true win-win for our world and our community. And with those win-wins, you feel joy from helping, and the person being helped feels happiness both from the result of the help and also from the fact that you wanted to and chose to help them. Both of you are enriched!

This is one key to growing into bliss. Once you have experienced this win-win joy, and repeat it, you will find it the single best method of adding more joy to your life.

It helps to think forward to a time, decades from now, when you will be reflecting on your life. Which items or measures will you be thinking about in considering what you have done with your life? Make a list of what you expect you'll be thinking at that point.

Review this list regularly. What will you be measuring at that point to determine how you've done?

Discern what excites and drives you. What things would you love to do? What do you love to create or accomplish? Here are my personal answers to this:

I personally happen to be driven by:

- Knowing I can change the way things are and improve lives
- Knowing I can make the world better
- Knowing I can bring more love into the lives of those I touch

- Knowing that to create these positive improvements, I must take actions
- Knowing that my time on earth is finite, so I'm motivated to create all the positive change I can in the time I have

Your chosen path may be a path less traveled, but that will make you a distinctive individual, so don't travel the path that is popular, but the path that calls you.

THE THREE SECRETS TO FULFILLMENT

For fulfillment, the first key is love. This includes exuding love to those around you and absorbing their love. Deep, loving connections are the most valuable things in life. Additionally, to enjoy your relationships deeply, you must give up wanting to be right. Recognize that. To change, first catch yourself wanting to be right when talking with someone. Then force yourself to let it go, because you now recognize it is seriously harming your relationships. Your loving relationships will become much more loving, and your friendships more peaceful and joyful!

Second is gratitude. Every day, feel gratitude for numerous things and show gratitude by helping other people. Gratitude brings growth and joy. Find gratitude for every little thing in your life; be appreciative of all. The opposite is entitlement—entitlement leads to unhappiness; drop that completely and feel grateful for everything that supports your life: each piece of food, the floor you walk, each piece of clothing you own, each day you get to live and decide what you'll do.

Third is forgiveness; forgiving yourself, your mistakes, and shortcomings—and loving yourself. Forgiveness cuts the rope that holds you back. You can fly forward! You may not condone what people did in the past, but you give it zero mental energy, knowing the future is all you can change.

Love
Feel the *love* around you.
Exude *love* around you.
Gratitude
Feel grateful for numerous "small" things.
Help others significantly.
Forgiveness
Forgive yourself.
Forgive others.

To really lift yourself up, your behavior should be consistent with your self-beliefs and values. When your behaviors match your beliefs about yourself, you will find more happiness, more loving connections with others, and your stress or tension will diminish. In thinking about how we would like to be, we should not hold ourselves to being saints, *but* should instead ask, "Which behaviors will make me feel best once they are done?" And not all of those behaviors need be saintly. Admit to yourself how you really want to be! Do not feel guilty about the ways you're different than a mythical saint. That guilt would be an anchor holding you back from being and living your best life, which means acting in consistency with your own beliefs about yourself.

Do not judge yourself; simply compare your actions to what you believe yourself to be. Judging is negative, degrading of yourself. Judging yourself becomes an anchor holding you back from what you can be. Comparing your actions against who you really are is a positive step moving you more quickly toward who you wish to become.

TREAT YOURSELF TO A GREAT LIFE

As you live using the lessons from this book and continue the journey from personal success to happiness and fulfillment, there is one more important area to understand. It's something you will experience—a strong desire to understand why you are on earth, what your life's large purpose is.

Happiness is nice, *but* there is deeper satisfaction available in life that comes from helping others, improving the circumstances of others, in ways that are consistent with the purpose you have discovered for your life. That purpose is different for everyone; it's very individual, but it can be a huge motivating force in guiding your actions and behaviors to generate success in the areas you care deeply about. People discover many different life purposes: helping others through health care, teaching, or being a fireman; starting and building successful companies as an entrepreneur; enjoying succeeding as a team with their workplace colleagues; serving as a priest, minister, or rabbi; working as a psychologist, helping individuals with problems or family situations; or being an artist, producing works of beauty and raising questions about life through art. The possibilities are almost as numerous as the number of people on the planet. But the important thing is to find, identify, and connect with your individual purpose. This is what will lead you to an even higher level of satisfaction, fulfillment, and joy. And once you know your purpose, to achieve the positive benefits I mentioned, you must do one thing more. You must spend your time as consistently as possible with your purpose in life.

As we do this, joy begins growing. From where it emanates most strongly is where we can concentrate our efforts to create deeper, more lasting joy, which also leads to closer, more meaningful connections with people we touch. This and your love of and connection with your family members offer the source of the most profound joy and satisfaction possible.

Although our world would be almost perfect if all 7.8 billion people on earth were filled with love, that is currently a dream. Our societal issues are long-standing, and I've reflected on how I understand our deep problems and our opportunities. At the core is the need to transform hate into love and hostility into positivity.

More Love and Positivity, Less Hostility and Hate

The we-they divided and hateful nature of our U.S. political activities and uncivil behavior are anguishing to most people, including myself.

Although there are numerous changes that might help, I believe the single biggest one is the following: when each of us realizes that our life's happiness exactly matches the amount of love and positivity we feel in our life, we will choose to feel love and positivity much more of the time and to allow ourselves to feel hostility and hate less of the time. When many in communities choose to enjoy love and positivity much more of the time, the feelings displayed in our politics will become less negative, more respectful of others holding different opinions, and less fractious. This will also help our communities and individual lives in many ways.

Each of us can lift our happiness by concentrating on how much of the time we are behaving out of love and positivity—and feeling love—and gradually intentionally increasing that time. As more of us do this, we can enjoy watching our society's health improve.

The Value and Equality of Each Person

My personal most important understanding is what I call my first recognition, and it's this: in the eyes of God and the universe, the life of each person on Earth has the same value as my life or your life. No matter how bad a person is, or how poor they are, or how aged, ill, or mean, their life has the exact same importance as mine. This drives not just my attitude toward each person, but much of my behavior and actions.

I occasionally consider, "How well am I doing at behaving consistently with that recognition?" I realize that the more I allow this recognition of individuals' equivalence and value to guide my actions and thoughts, the happier and more enthused about life I am.

So, how are we doing as a society and a country? We have a long way to go. But while it's a significant journey, the payoff can be enormous. For me, this is not a commandment, but it is a recognition—the recognition that you and I are not more important than any other individual on Earth. This has great power and implications for life and happiness. It also determines who we will be as a society.

When a person believes in the equality and unity of all persons, one understands that helping others is as important as helping oneself.

173

Selfishness wanes as a person sees and grasps easy ways to help other people, and the understanding grows that while I'm not as certain how to improve my own life, I can see simple ways to end suffering by others, and to improve their well-being. In fact, the answer to how to improve your own life is exactly this: seeing how to improve others' lives and actively doing it. This is the most powerful way to improve your own life. Once you understand these precepts and act accordingly, there is no more mystery about how to improve your own joy and fulfillment—you will see that it just happens, and you will be amazed at how improved your own life is. I have found no other way to create permanent joy than this. Happiness is otherwise temporary and fleeting, but the joy from recognizing the importance of others, and helping them improve their lives and their happiness, is permanent and doesn't waver. You can feel this joy every day, forever.

The evil behaviors, schisms, and hate sometimes among us or within America are foundationally explained by the lack of: belief or acknowledgment that we are each of the same value and importance, and the paucity of positive helping behavior in our society, a behavior that is missing because of not understanding these simple truths. As a society, we can positively transform by understanding the equality of others and accepting and leading our personal lives based on these understandings. When many of us grow into this wonderful realization and act accordingly, our society can become positively transformed.

You can create a life beyond your dreams by using the powers and magic available to design, effectuate, and live enthusiastically. Love your life! Enjoy your future!

Our book's end—your beginning!

ACKNOWLEDGMENTS

For this becoming publishable, all credit goes to Tim Brandhorst with Marc J. Lane,

To the extent this flows as enjoyable reading, all credit goes to my remarkable and wonderful wife Iliana, who also inspired me to persevere and dig deeper in seeking truths,

To the extent this improves innumerable lives, all credit goes to Post Hill Press, especially Heather King and Debby Englander,

To the extent this imparts valuable life lessons, I thank and appreciate all individuals I have worked with, and will in the future work with, in our wonderful companies—they have taught me what I know,

To the extent this inspires younger persons to believe in greatness for their lives, credit goes to my positively energizing daughters Monique, Charlotte, and Alicia.